The BERA Guide to Practitioner Research

The BERA Guides

Critical Insights into Educational Research and Practice

About the Series

Published in partnership between the British Educational Research Association and Emerald Publishing, *The BERA Guides* are short, research-informed yet accessible introductions to key, interdisciplinary topics impacting education research and practice.

Books in the series present a summary of the research on the topic, charting how scholarly thought and practice have evolved over time, and offering critical takeaways and suggestions for future work within and beyond academia. With the guides viewed as 'primers' on each topic, the series is for use by a broad academic audience, including early career and established researchers, postgraduate students and practitioners.

Published in the Series

The BERA Guide to Mental Health and Wellbeing in Schools: Exploring Frontline Support in Educational Research and Practice; *Edited by Michelle Jayman, Jonathan Glazzard, Anthea Rose and Aimee Quickfall*

The BERA Guide to Decolonising the Curriculum: Equity and Inclusion in Educational Research and Practice; *Edited by Marlon Lee Moncrieffe, Omolabake Fakunle, Marlies Kustatscher and Anna Olsson Rost*

The BERA Guide to Outdoor Learning: Place-Responsive Pedagogy in Educational Research and Practice; *Edited by Lucy Sors and Ruth Unsworth*

Forthcoming in the Series

The BERA Guide to Environmental and Sustainability Education: Creating Just Futures in Educational Research and Practice; *Edited by Elizabeth Rushton and Lynda Dunlop*

The BERA Guide to Implementing Inclusive Education: Understanding SEND in UK Educational Research and Practice; *Edited by Rhiannon Packer*

The BERA Guide to Climate Change Education: Systemic Approaches in Educational Research and Practice; *Authored by Dima Khazem*

The BERA Guide to Social Justice-Oriented Leadership: Connections and Implications in Educational Research and Practice; *Authored by Liliana Belkin and Deborah A. Sabric*

The BERA Guide to Practitioner Research

Developing Professional Knowledge in Educational Research and Practice

Edited by

Kate Mawson
Nottingham Trent University, UK

Claire Haresnape Tyson
Homewood School and Sixth Form Centre, UK

Thomas Perry
University of Warwick, UK

and

Joyce I-Hui Chen
College of West Anglia, UK

United Kingdom – North America – Japan – India
Malaysia – China

Emerald Publishing Limited
Emerald Publishing, Floor 5, Northspring, 21-23 Wellington Street, Leeds LS1 4DL.

First edition 2026

Editorial matter and selection © 2026 Kate Mawson, Claire Haresnape Tyson, Thomas Perry, and Joyce I-Hui Chen.
Individual chapters © 2026 The authors.
Published under exclusive licence by Emerald Publishing Limited.

Reprints and permissions service
Contact: www.copyright.com

No part of this book may be reproduced, stored in a retrieval system, transmitted in any form or by any means electronic, mechanical, photocopying, recording or otherwise without either the prior written permission of the publisher or a licence permitting restricted copying issued in the UK by The Copyright Licensing Agency and in the USA by The Copyright Clearance Center. Any opinions expressed in the chapters are those of the authors. Whilst Emerald makes every effort to ensure the quality and accuracy of its content, Emerald makes no representation implied or otherwise, as to the chapters' suitability and application and disclaims any warranties, express or implied, to their use.

British Library Cataloguing in Publication Data
A catalogue record for this book is available from the British Library

ISBN: 978-1-83608-963-6 (Print)
ISBN: 978-1-83608-960-5 (Online)
ISBN: 978-1-83608-962-9 (Epub)

INVESTOR IN PEOPLE

Contents

About the Editors — xi

About the Contributors — xiii

Introduction and Editorial Perspective on Practitioner Research — 1
Thomas Perry and Claire Haresnape Tyson

INTRODUCTION TO SECTION 1: THE FIELD OF PRACTITIONER RESEARCH AND WORLDVIEWS
Thomas Perry and Claire Haresnape Tyson

Chapter 1 – Practitioner Research in Education: Philosophical Foundations, Contextual Applications, and Policy Implications — 15
Holly Heshmati

Chapter 2 – Practitioner Research in Initial Teacher Education — 23
Vicky Christoforatou

Chapter 3 – Bridging the Gap: Enhancing Research-Practice Links in Education for a Research-Informed Future — 31
Adriane Martini

INTRODUCTION TO SECTION 2: POWER, POSITIONALITY, AND IDENTITY IN PRACTITIONER RESEARCH
Kate Mawson

Chapter 4 – Empowering a Research-Engaged Profession — 43
Rachel Marsden and Gillian Peiser

Chapter 5 – The Cyclical Nature of Being Both 'Practitioner' and 'Researcher' and the Influence on Professional Development Design — 51
Rebekah Gear and Tazreen Kassim-Lowe

Chapter 6 – Three Lecturers, Three Universities, Three Countries: Can Facilitating Connecting Art Workshops in International Educational Contexts Create Connection and Criticality?   61
Frances-Ann Norton

Chapter 7 – Researching on the Inside Looking in: Navigating Issues of Power in Conducting Practitioner Research Projects   71
Sarah Peters and Joyce I-Hui Chen

Chapter 8 – Teachers Teaching Teachers   79
Sylvia Ikomi

INTRODUCTION TO SECTION 3: PROFESSIONAL LEARNING AND SHARING SKILLS
Joyce I-Hui Chen

Chapter 9 – The Journey Towards a Whole-School Culture of Teachers as Researchers: Reflections from a State-Maintained School for Students with Special Educational Needs and Disabilities   91
Hannah Lovatt and Gina Stafford

Chapter 10 – Developing Research-Informed Trainee Teachers   101
Elizabeth Hidson

Chapter 11 – Disrupting to Develop   109
Debbie Bogard, Freya Cox-Willmott and Neil Hart

Chapter 12 – Developing Professional Knowledge as a Consortium: Moving from 'I' to 'We'   117
The RATED Consortium consisting of: Claire Haresnape Tyson, Matthew J. Easterbrook, Lewis Doyle, Alison Glover, Elizabeth Hidson and Thomas Perry

Chapter 13 – An Insider Perspective: Exploring Teachers' Engagement with Professional Development in Cooperation with Practitioner Co-Researchers   125
Marianne Talbot

Chapter 14 – The Research-Engaged Practitioner: The Importance of Research Literacy and Critical Reflection for the Novice Teacher's Professional Learning   135
Leanne Henderson, Danyah Alsayeud and Ian Collen

INTRODUCTION TO SECTION 4: RESEARCH KNOWLEDGE, QUALITY, AND ETHICS IN PRACTITIONER RESEARCH
Kate Mawson

Chapter 15 – How the Quality of Research and Research Partnerships (Practitioner Researcher) Can Be Enhanced by Using Critical Theory as a Framework 145
Kate Newby, Matthew Lee and Amanda Lee

Chapter 16 – Unpacking and Underpinning the Ethical Conduct and Sharing of Practitioner Research 155
Alison Twiner, Patrick Carmichael, Pete Dudley, Sara Hennessy and Ying Ji

Chapter 17 – Exploratory Practice: What About the Learners? 163
Rachel Bate

Chapter 18 – Managing Ethical Dilemmas with the Dual Identity of Practitioner and Researcher 171
John Parkin

Chapter 19 – Dialogical Knowledge Curation in Education: Integrating Research and Practice in North East Wales 179
Tomos G. ap Sion, Lisa Formby, Sue Horder and Karen Rhys Jones

Chapter 20 – Reflections and Future Directions in Practitioner Research 189
Kate Mawson, Thomas Perry, Claire Haresnape Tyson and Joyce I-Hui Chen

Glossary 199

Index 213

About the Editors

Dr Kate Mawson is an internationally recognised advocate for practitioner research in education, known for bridging rigorous academic inquiry with professional practice. Across a career spanning more than 25 years, she has worked as an Associate Professor in Russell Group universities, post-92 institutions, and both state and independent school sectors. Her sustained involvement in teacher education, from initial teacher training to postgraduate supervision and colleague development and mentoring, underpins her commitment to developing research-literate educators. Holding a Professional Doctorate in Education, Dr Mawson has published widely on practitioner research and evidence-informed pedagogy. Her work foregrounds the role of inquiry as a driver of professional learning and systemic change.

Dr Claire Haresnape Tyson is a teacher researcher based at Homewood School and Sixth Form Centre, where she combines teaching science and the extended project qualification (EPQ) with her research role. She is currently Principal Teacher of Sixth Form with responsibility for Raising Standards (Maternity Cover). Her PhD was obtained by studying part-time with Queen Mary, University of London in Clinical Pharmacology. Her research role includes working with school staff and students to develop academic writing, academic integrity and research capacity in the school. She is a founding member of the RATED consortium (Research informed Approaches to Tackling Educational Disadvantage), a research partnership of academics and teachers focused on improving outcomes for students through collaborative research opportunities. She was a co-convenor of the BERA Special Interest Group for Practitioner Research from 2018 to 2024. This opportunity has led to publications and writing partnerships with a wide range of academics and practitioners. In 2025, she achieved her National Professional Qualification in Leading Teacher Development.

Dr Thomas Perry is a social scientist, education researcher and educator. He works at the intersection of research, policy and practice, with a focus on generating and applying evidence to address real-world challenges in education. He is Reader in Education Studies and Director of Postgraduate Research in the School of Education, Learning and Communication Sciences at the University of Warwick.

Dr Joyce I-Hui Chen is Quality Enhancement Manager and Centre Manager for Initial Teacher Education. She has been working in different educational sectors for more than 20 years in Taiwan and in the United Kingdom (UK), from primary education to higher education. Her current job role includes initial teacher education, organisational development and teachers' professional development and learning in a general further education college in England. She has undertaken several practitioner research projects over the last 10 years in the further education sector. Her main research interests are FE policies, practice-focused professional development and learning and ethical practice. She is passionate about connecting and collaborating with practitioners across different educational sectors and has been supporting practitioners with research. She has co-founded a research and innovation forum to engage with internal and external colleagues who can exchange knowledge and research.

About the Contributors

Danyah Alsayeud is an experienced EFL practitioner who has taught at King Abdulaziz University and the University of Jeddah. Her research focuses on improving EFL students' writing skills and teacher reflection. She is currently undertaking a PhD at Queen's University Belfast, investigating Reflective Practice amongst Lecturers in the Saudi EFL context.

Tomos G. ap Sion is an early-career researcher and PhD candidate (University of St Andrews) supporting research in the social sciences at Wrexham University (Wales, UK). His work in education has spanned a number of topics, including community schools, embedding research and enquiry in schools, and practitioner pedagogical development. His primary research interests lie in the nature of science and promoting scientific progress, with numerous publications in the social sciences, psychology, and the philosophy of science.

Rachel Bate is an experienced ESOL tutor working in Adult and Community Learning in London. She completed a PhD considering pedagogical approaches to developing learners' voices drawing on the work of Mikhael Bakhtin. Through her research, she has become interested in methods which have the potential to promote learner agency and encourage collaborative working.

Debbie Bogard has taught history and politics for over two decades in schools and sixth form colleges. Debbie leads on teacher development and practitioner research in her current Further Education (FE) role. She also works in the British Library Learning Team, running workshops for school groups, and continuing professional development (CPD) for trainees and practicing teachers. She is particularly interested in non-positional, collaborative leadership, and supporting teachers through a shared love of learning.

Camtree (the Cambridge Teacher Research Exchange) are a team of academics and practitioners based at Hughes Hall and the Faculty of Education, University of Cambridge. With many years' experience working with and as practitioners, we are seeking to develop system-level enablers to challenges of sharing and learning from practitioner research.

Dr Patrick Carmichael's research has explored the intersections between teacher learning and information systems, and the potential of digital technologies to enhance teaching, learning and research. As Managing Director of Camtree, he leads the development of Camtree's unique digital library in line with 'open research' principles.

Vicky Christoforatou is a Lecturer in Education on the Secondary PGCE English Course. Her priorities include the promotion of effective mentoring provision for trainee teachers and the professional development of school mentors. In her own research, she explores English teachers' approaches to the teaching of writing in secondary schools.

Ian Collen is Director of Initial Teacher Education at Queen's University Belfast, where he teaches in the field of Modern Languages Education. He has led research projects funded by the British Academy and the British Council. His teaching ensures emerging teachers are reflective practitioners confident in leading learning in research-informed classrooms.

Freya Cox-Willmott is subject lead for A level Sociology at a large north London sixth form college. She considers herself a learner first, and a teacher second. Freya is particularly interested in interdisciplinary education, collaborative practice, creating communities of practice across a wide range of teaching spaces and disrupting power hierarchies in spaces of learning. She is soon to start a Master's in Gender and Sexuality studies at Birkbeck University.

Lewis Doyle is a Senior Postdoctoral Researcher at the Université de Poitiers, France, and Visiting Researcher at the School of Psychology. His research uses social psychology to highlight and combat educational and societal inequalities.

Dr Pete Dudley has substantial experience teaching and leading school improvement and teacher research, notably at England's National College for School Leadership and as Director of the Primary National Strategy. Now CEO of Camtree, Pete continues to work with teachers and leaders using lesson study to improve learning, teaching, and schools.

Matthew J. Easterbrook is a reader in social psychology at the University of Sussex. His research aims to increase our understanding of, and ability to reduce, educational, political, and economic inequality.

Lisa Formby is the Education Research Lead, overseeing and coordinating various research projects within the Education department in Wrexham University (Wales, UK). She leads the Community Schools research initiative and collaborates on multiple research teams exploring areas such as Talk Pedagogy, Embedding Research and Enquiry in Schools, and Trauma-Informed school approaches. Her research interests focus on educational inequalities affecting children and young people and health and wellbeing.

Rebekah Gear is a Lecturer in Primary Education at Nottingham Trent University. With a background in primary teaching and mathematics leadership, she specialises in inclusive pedagogy, curriculum design, and practitioner inquiry. Her work explores how engaging as both practitioner and researcher informs meaningful, research-led professional development in education.

Alison Glover is a Research Fellow on the Open University ITE Partnership PGCE programme in Wales. She has worked in all sectors of education from early years to higher education and has undertaken many research projects in the Welsh education context. Current research interests include teacher education and partnership working.

Neil Hart has taught Science and Biology A-level across inner-London schools and sixth form colleges for 20 years. He is interested in approaches that diversify understanding of the history and potential futures of biology. Neil is completing a PhD at King's College London, developing new pedagogies to support young Londoners from marginalised communities to live-well in times of social and ecological crises.

Leanne Henderson is Programme Director of BA Education Studies at Queen's University Belfast, and is a committed reflective practitioner who supports her students to engage critically with research evidence through their own reflective practice. Her research interests are in Modern Languages Education and Language Policy, Educational Equity and Children's Rights.

Sara Hennessy is Professor of Educational Dialogue and Pedagogical Inquiry in the Faculty of Education, University of Cambridge and Deputy CEO of Camtree, Hughes Hall. She is co-founder of the Cambridge Educational Dialogue Research (CEDiR) group. Her research focuses on classroom dialogue, educational technology and teacher professional development.

Dr Holly Heshmati is an Associate Professor at the University of Warwick. Her research focuses on initial teacher education and mathematics education. She has been involved in various practitioner research projects that explore innovative approaches to teacher education, aiming to improve engagement, motivation, and overall outcomes for both teachers and students.

Dr Elizabeth Hidson is a Senior Lecturer and Research and Knowledge Exchange Fellow at the University of Sunderland. She is co-founder of the InterAction research unit, dedicated to impactful research with schools and teachers. She is also an editor of the *Learning to Teach in the Secondary School* textbook, now in its 10th edition. She works with schools and teachers in over 60 countries, and is programme leader for the MA in International Education.

Dr Sue Horder is an Associate Dean (Academic Affairs) in the Faculty of Social and Life Sciences. Before coming to Wrexham University (Wales, UK), Sue's teaching career began in Further Education. Sue moved to a role in Higher Education in 2006 as a Senior Lecturer teaching on the PGCE/Cert Ed programme and other undergraduate and postgraduate programmes within Education, prior to becoming Associate Dean in 2016. Sue's research interests are around supporting the embedding of research and enquiry in schools, community schools, outdoor learning, and the influence of student teachers' epistemological beliefs on their conceptions of teaching and their classroom practice.

Sylvia Ikomi delivers Continuous Professional Development sessions to teachers and social workers aimed at addressing the issue of the adultification of Black girls. Sylvia Ikomi is the author of *Child Q: A Case Study of the Adultification of Black Girls in School* and *The Adultification of Black Girls in State Care: Perspectives*.

Dr Ying Ji is a Research Associate at Camtree, Hughes Hall, University of Cambridge. Her work focuses on teacher professional development, teacher-led inquiry, and research translation. She co-developed the Think-Talk Toolbox and leads international projects on dialogic learning and the development of transversal skills through practitioner-led inquiry.

Dr Karen Rhys Jones is a Principal Lecturer in Wrexham University (Wales, UK) and the Initial Teacher Education Lead; she leads the PGCE Primary Education Programme with QTS and is subject leader for physical education. Her research allows her to keep abreast of contemporary and current educational issues and support teaching and student learning. Karen is an active member of Wrexham University's Research group, working on a range of collaborative research projects and initiatives.

Amanda Lee is a Lecturer in the School of Nursing and Health Sciences at the University of Sunderland, and co-Chair of the UoS Family Staff Network. She has over 10 years' experience as an educator across primary, secondary and higher education. Her research focuses on inclusivity and emotionality in education.

Matthew Lee is a Senior Lecturer in CPD at the University of Sunderland, specialising in post-registration nurse education. A registered nurse with the NMC, he is co-Chair of the UoS Race, Ethnicity, and Cultural Heritage Staff Network. His research explores pedagogical strategies to challenge racial oppression and empower communities.

Hannah Lovatt is a Lecturer in Education at the University of Greater Manchester, specialising in inclusion and disability. She began her teaching career in the alternative schooling sector, primarily in autism-specific provision. In addition to her research interests in neuroinclusion and teacher-research, she is exploring how community-based research partnerships can serve to centre typically marginalised voices.

Tazreen Kassim-Lowe, formerly a primary school teacher and maths lead, is a Doctoral student at the University of Nottingham, where she also supports larger scale research projects. She works as a professional and school development lead for East Midlands West Mathshub.

Rachel Marsden is a University-Based Teacher Educator in Secondary English. She has previously taught English and Classical Civilisation in secondary schools and further education. Her PhD focused on research-informed practice as a way of empowering teachers to be active agents in the knowledge generation of their own profession.

Adriane Martini is currently working at a leading independent school in North London as Director of Teaching and Learning, Head of Research and A-level Psychology Teacher. In the role as Head of Research, she conducts academic studies to support the school's pedagogical development, disseminating findings through CPD sessions and publishing an annual research journal with contributions from colleagues, as well as seeking to connect with other researchers across the world. She has just completed most recent academic journey at Oxford University, where she earned an MSc in Teacher Education. Her interests lie primarily at the intersection of philosophy, psychology, and education, whether in exploring ideas in the academic realm or experimenting with them in her teaching practices.

Kate Newby is the Faculty Academic Support Lead for Nursing & Midwifery at the University of Sunderland and Head of its Centre for Inclusive Learning. With over 15 years in Higher Education, she oversees quality in programmes for health professionals. Her research focuses on inclusive education and supporting diverse student communities.

Frances-Ann Norton is a practice-focused educational researcher and an artist educator. Her research is influenced by constructivist paradigms in Dewey's experiential learning and Bernstein's Pedagogic Rights. She lectures in art and teacher training. She has given papers at international conferences and has been published in academic journals and book chapters.

John Parkin was a primary school teacher for 15 years mostly teaching Reception-aged children before joining Anglia Ruskin University as a Senior Lecturer Practitioner in 2018. His own career as a male primary school teacher led to his interest in the experiences and motivations of men joining a BA Primary Education Studies degree, which led to his doctoral research. As well as research interests examining masculinities, John has investigated co-creation with students and playful approaches to learning.

Gillian Peiser is a Senior Lecturer in Teacher Education at Liverpool John Moores University (LJMU). She leads the PGCE in Modern Languages, is Deputy Director of the Liverpool Institute for Educational Research and supervises doctoral students. Gillian researches the role of research in teachers' professional learning, mentoring, and intercultural learning.

Sarah Peters is a Lecturer in Teacher Education, Learning and Skills Research Network regional convenor and Society for Education and Training Practitioner Advisory Group member. RATED is the acronym for Research-informed Approaches to Tackling Educational Disadvantage, a consortium of academics, teachers, and educators who collaboratively work together to reduce educational inequalities and disadvantages using evidence-based approaches.

Gina Stafford is a Senior Leader at a large secondary school for learners with Special Educational Needs and Disabilities (SEND), where she leads on Teaching, Learning, Research, Initial Teacher Training and Continuous Professional Development. Currently completing a Doctorate in Education, Gina combines academic research with practical expertise to drive meaningful improvements within her school and in the local community. Gina is a keen advocate of system leadership, championing collaboration and the sharing of best practice across schools and local partnerships. Her belief in research-informed strategies and collective responsibility underpins her mission to enhance life chances for the most vulnerable learners; ensuring every child has access to high-quality, equitable education.

Marianne Talbot is a PhD researcher, investigating the impact of professional development in educational assessment on qualified teachers and their assessment practice. She is an Academic Personal Tutor, a Chartered Educational Assessor, a Fellow of the Chartered Institute of Educational Assessors, and a Fellow of the Higher Education Academy.

Dr Alison Twiner is a Senior Research Associate at Camtree. Her interests are particularly in understanding multimodal communication to support meaning making and learning; alongside supporting practitioners and settings to explore and adapt their practices, and to share practitioner-authored insights to benefit the wider education community.

Introduction and Editorial Perspective on Practitioner Research

Thomas Perry[a] *and Claire Haresnape Tyson*[b]
[a]*University of Warwick, UK*
[b]*Homewood School and Sixth Form Centre, UK*

Introducing This Book

This edited collection brings together a diverse set of practitioner researchers who offer insights grounded in their own professional settings, challenges, and priorities. At its heart, this book is a contribution to the growing body of work that takes practitioner research (PR) seriously – not only as a methodological stance, but as a way of knowing, acting, and enriching education.

Our aim is to foreground PR as a meaningful, rigorous, and impactful approach to inquiry. Across the chapters, contributors explore the possibilities and constraints of conducting research from within their professional roles, bringing attention to both the richness and complexity of practitioner-led inquiry. In doing so, the book offers a window into the realities of researching practice from within, often with the intention of improving that very practice.

We are particularly concerned with fostering dialogue around three core questions:

- What counts as PR?
- What values and purposes underpin it?
- How can PR contribute to educational knowledge and change?

The chapters that follow do not offer a singular answer to these questions. Instead, they offer a multiplicity of perspectives – shaped by context, role, discipline, and purpose – which, we believe, is both necessary and valuable. We see this diversity not as a limitation but as a hallmark of the field.

Purpose and Ethos

The impetus behind this book was to create a space where practitioner researchers could reflect on their work in ways that are theoretically grounded, methodologically sound, and personally and professionally meaningful. We wanted to create a collection that is both practical and provocative – one that can support others engaging in PR, while also asking difficult and generative questions about its assumptions, boundaries, and contributions.

From the outset, we have treated this as a collaborative and dialogic endeavour. We began by sharing with contributors our editorial perspective on PR – the central section of this chapter – and invited them to respond, reflect, or critique its assumptions and arguments in their own chapters. In this way, the book becomes a conversation: between editors and contributors, between different professional communities, and between theory and practice.

In shaping the book, we also embraced a level of heterogeneity – in both voice and style – that reflects the field's diversity. Rather than impose a uniform tone or structure, we aimed to honour the situatedness of each contributor's voice. The editorial process involved read-through sessions, group meetings, and feedback loops that allowed for both individual expression and collective shaping. We resisted the temptation to produce a 'textbook' that reduces everything to a single understanding. Instead, we have created a glossary to support readers in navigating the variety of terms used, without insisting on a single, homogeneous vocabulary. In doing so, we acknowledge that PR, like the communities it represents, thrives on difference, dialogue, and contextual meaning-making.

In curating this volume, we were guided by a set of shared commitments:

- To value the knowledge produced in practice, by practitioners, for practitioners and the communities they serve.
- To recognise the diversity of PR traditions, purposes, and philosophical commitments.
- To maintain a focus on ethical, contextually grounded, and reflexive forms of inquiry.
- To highlight both the possibilities and the tensions involved in occupying the dual identity of practitioner and researcher.

We hope this collection serves not only as a resource but also as a stimulus to think differently about the role of practitioners in educational research, and to affirm their place as legitimate, capable, and creative knowledge-makers.

PR: An Editorial Perspective

As the first step in the collaborative process of writing this book, we, the editors, developed and then shared our perspectives on PR as a form of inquiry. Our contributing authors were asked to include their responses and reflections on our perspective in their chapters. This was intended to be a way to create a meta-cognitive level of understanding that we could use to connect with each other and to have useful discussions.

Taking a historical perspective, we can see that over the years, PR has been 'shaped and reshaped in relation to the era within which it has existed' (Dana, 2016, p. 1). We have come a long way since Stenhouse noted the reluctance of educational researchers to engage teachers as partners in, and critics of, the research process (Stenhouse, 1985, p. 1).

Currently, there is an interest in 'close-to-practise research'[1] and Parsons emphasises the central importance of collaboration to the generation of knowledge (Parsons, 2021, p. 1490). While there may be an assumption in CtP that academic knowledge is separate from practice and can be 'transferred' to bring about improvements, it is also possible to create collaborative partnerships where knowledge is shared or exchanged. A common barrier to such work may be differences in epistemological biases and stances, but discussion of these could create more coherence and enrich understanding between parties.

Our starting point is that PR is research done by practitioners for practical purposes. The nature of education means that practitioners deal with the complex, dynamic and messy issues of practical action. A curious and reflective teacher can hardly avoid asking themselves 'What is happening here?', 'What should and can I do to make this better?', and 'What will best achieve my aims?'. When that inquiry becomes sustained, self-critical, systematic and/or shared (Stenhouse, 1985, p. 18), we can say it starts to take the form of research (Stenhouse, 1981, p. 103; also see Cochran-Smith & Lytle, 1993, pp. 23–24).

Philosophical Worldview

PR is, by definition, closely linked to action and therefore naturally lends itself to pragmatic philosophical positions. Much PR is rooted in the work of John Dewey and the belief that practitioners are both 'consumers' and 'producers' of knowledge (Cochran-Smith & Lytle, 1993, p. 9). What does Dewey's pragmatism have to offer us? He provides an account of knowledge and an understanding of the way in which human beings can acquire knowledge that differs from philosophies focused on generalisation, abstraction and representation. He deals with questions of knowledge and the acquisition of knowledge within a framework of a philosophy of action. Human action is always the interactions between elements of human nature and the environment both natural and social. This transactional approach (Biesta & Burbules, 2003, p. 10) where reality reveals itself as a result of these interactions allows knowledge to be both constructed and based on reality.

PR has an affinity to but is not limited to pragmatist research philosophy and methodology. Practitioners have the philosophical freedom to embrace other philosophies, including positivist and constructionist forms of knowledge. The purpose for PR is that research is applied. This allows for pluralism and calls for what Biesta (2020) describes as being pragmatic without being a pragmatist. We are not saying that we should sidestep the debates about the values of different forms of knowledge, that debate is both healthy and necessary and fosters collaborative partnerships, but we are saying that we can consciously avoid taking up a position that is too fixed and therefore self-limiting.

Methodology

There is a strong tradition of PR being framed as action research (Finch, 2022). Our position is that being a practitioner researcher often involves action research but that the role will benefit from engaging with a range of research methodologies and skills. The ability to choose the most appropriate method for the practical problem in focus is consistent with the pragmatic worldview and the variety of hierarchical positions and different roles that Practitioner Researchers may occupy in their institutions.

Adopting Mixed Methods Research (MMR) is also common as it allows the PR to choose from both qualitative and quantitative methods, utilising those tools and methods that best suit their inquiry. By remaining in a state of neutrality in the 'paradigm wars' (Johnson & Onwuegbuzie, 2004, p. 14) and taking a pluralistic approach PR can conduct more effective research especially in interdisciplinary and complex situations.

Typical responsibilities that we have been able to identify from our own experience, reading and engagement with the BERA SIG community[2] include:

- Developing a methodology and philosophical worldview as a basis for research in one's own practice.
- Acknowledging and giving voice to the different perspectives that are operating within an institution.
- Embedding ethical research practices within an institution.

- Upholding academic integrity and academic honesty in a community and in personal practice.
- Supporting colleagues to become critical and reflective in their practice and/or research.
- Measuring, describing, and evaluating the impact of what is happening in an institution.
- Building outward facing links with academic institutions and the wider research community.
- Communicating and sharing results with the students, staff, and parents.
- Publishing and disseminating research to the wider community.
- Contributing to the professional development of colleagues and students by sharing and fostering research skills and research knowledge.
- Being aware of the educational research landscape and how different organisations or institutions hold differing views on implementing what works.

Ethics, Power, and Positionality

Power is an important consideration for PR, in terms of the legitimacy and resource for different forms of research in education and in terms of how the practitioner researcher is situated in and interacts with their immediate and wider community. A practitioner researcher may be working at leadership level, as a classroom teacher or a teacher trainee. As well as their hierarchical position in their own context, practitioner researchers occupy a 'third space' (Ostinelli, 2016, p. 542) between the worlds of academic knowledge and practical knowledge. This requires them to acknowledge and value differing forms of evidence ranging from individual experiences and local understandings to wider, more universally accepted findings from educational research. The ability to think critically about the utility of both forms of knowledge is a key skill for conducting research that has both impact and rigour.

There is also a need to think critically about ethics and values and adopt a consonant form of research practice. The distinction between procedural ethics (what researchers are told by HEIs that they need to do) and ethics-in-practice (what researchers do in the field) is an interesting point that we invite you to explore. PR is also connected to values that are inherent to the role of practitioner and that these need to be explicitly acknowledged. 'Living with the consequences of research makes practitioner researchers more conscientious about values in relation to current research participants and the future impact of their work' (Fox et al., 2007, p. 197).

PR as Unsettled and Evolving

With this clarification of our own understanding of what it means to be a Practitioner Researcher, we offered an opportunity for our contributors to respond with their own viewpoints and their critique of our vision of PR that is substantially rooted in a pragmatist worldview. 'The role is underpinned by reflexivity that comes from the proximity of the practitioner to the field of research' (Fox et al., 2007, p. 196). Reflexivity recognises that there is a continuous exchange between the researcher, the researched and the research which is fundamental to the action research. As such, reflexivity should be incorporated into the research in a systematic and rigorous manner.

Our view is that it is a dynamic and evolving role that reflects the changes to the profession and discipline as well as the unique requirements of each context. Today, some of the shared characteristics include collegiate relationships between practitioner researchers and participants; emancipatory practices; and the transformational agency of practitioner researchers. It is our hope that the different contributors to this book will illustrate many of these characteristics and bring them to life for us.

Concluding Thoughts: Themes and Trajectories

This book is intended as both an invitation and a challenge: an invitation to engage with the richly varied practices of PR, and a challenge to take seriously its potential to shape educational thinking, policy, and practice from within.

Across the chapters, our contributors examine PR from multiple vantage points. The book is structured around four key themes that emerged from our editorial conversations and the submitted chapters – themes that we believe offer a coherent yet expansive way to explore the field.

- **Section 1** addresses *the field of PR and its associated worldviews*. Here, contributors grapple with foundational questions about what PR is, why it matters, and how different philosophical and methodological positions influence the way we do and understand this work.

- **Section 2** explores *identity, power, and positionality*. These chapters examine what it means to research from within – negotiating roles, relationships, and responsibilities. They foreground questions of legitimacy, agency, and the ethical tensions that arise when the researcher is also a colleague, leader, or learner in the field they study.

- **Section 3** focuses on *professional learning and the sharing of skills*. These chapters illustrate the ways PR can foster collaborative cultures, build capacity, and support the development of research-informed practice. They highlight how research can become a shared endeavour, embedded in professional communities.

- **Section 4** turns to *research knowledge and research quality, including ethics*. Here, contributors consider the standards by which PR is judged, the diverse forms of knowledge it generates, and the ethical imperatives of working in ways that are both contextually sensitive and methodologically rigorous.

Throughout the book, readers will encounter examples of research that is both deeply embedded in professional settings and shaped by broader theoretical and ethical concerns. We hope these chapters provoke critical engagement, spark new questions, and inspire further research by and with practitioners.

This book does not attempt to define PR once and for all – nor should it. Instead, we hope it offers a map of a rich and evolving terrain, and encourages others to add their own paths, landmarks, and perspectives to the journey.

Notes

1. https://www.bera.ac.uk/publication/bera-statement-on-close-to-practice-research
2. https://www.bera.ac.uk/community/practitioner-research 02/02/24

References

Biesta, G. (2020). *Educational research: An unorthodox introduction*. Bloomsbury Academic.

Biesta, G., & Burbules, N. C. (2003). *Pragmatism and educational research*. Rowman & Littlefield.

Cochran-Smith, M., & Lytle, S. L. (Eds.). (1993). *Inside/outside: Teacher research and Knowledge*. Teachers College Press.

Dana, N. F. (2016). The relevancy and importance of practitioner research in contemporary times. *Journal of Practitioner Research*, 1(1), 1. http://doi.org/10.5038/2379-9951.1.1.1034

Finch, M. (2022). Complexities of practitioner research: Seeking hallmarks of quality. *Impacting Education: Journal on Transforming Professional Practice*, 7(3), 1–10.

Fox, M., Green, G., & Martin, P. (2007). *Doing practitioner research*. SAGE Publications.

Johnson, R. B., & Onwuegbuzie, A. J. (2004). Mixed methods research: A research paradigm whose time has come. *Educational Researcher*, 33(7), 14–26. https://doi.org/10.3102/0013189X033007014

Ostinelli, G. (2016). The many forms of research-informed practice: A framework for mapping diversity. *European Journal of Teacher Education*, 39(5), 534–549. http://dx.doi.org/10.1080/02619768.2016.1252913]

Parsons, S. (2021). The importance of collaboration for knowledge co-construction in 'close-to-practice' research. *British Educational Research Journal*, 47(6), 1490–1499.

Stenhouse, L. (1981). What counts as research? *British Journal of Educational Studies*, 29(2), 103–114. https://doi.org/10.1080/00071005.1981.9973589

Stenhouse, L. (1985). *Research as a basis for teaching: Readings from the work of Lawrence Stenhouse* (J. Rudduck & D. Hopkins, Eds.). Heinemann Educational Books.

Introduction to Section 1: The Field of Practitioner Research and Worldviews

Thomas Perry[a] and Claire Haresnape Tyson[b]
[a]*University of Warwick, UK*
[b]*Homewood School and Sixth Form Centre, UK*

Introduction

Practitioner research (PR) is conducted by and for a wide range of people working in education, with a number of complex and developed philosophical worldviews. The complexity comes not from an elaborate theoretical system or research methodology, but from the ongoing preoccupation with relating theory, evidence and practice. Practitioner researchers both conduct and apply research, and must develop as they do a rich understanding of how research and the knowledge it produces can form and inform practice.

In Section 1, we explore key ideas in the field of PR. The contributions chosen for this section have a focus on philosophical worldview, many drawing on the ideas and democratic ethos of pragmatism as they ask what drives research and what are the processes involved? The chapters also shed light on how and why PR may vary in different settings.

Here, we make some introductory remarks, commenting on each chapter in relation to the editorial, and how each author helps us to develop our PR worldview.

The chapter 'Practitioner Research in Education: Philosophical Foundations, Contextual Applications, and Policy Implications' by Holly Heshmati contributes to the discourse by emphasising the value of PR as a valuable form of knowledge creation, challenging the traditional dominance of academic-led research. It highlights the importance of practitioners' lived experiences and insights and provides specific insights into how PR can be used to develop teacher resilience, a crucial factor in teacher retention and quality education. She argues that PR can generate valuable evidence-based insights to inform policy decisions, ensuring that policies are grounded in real-world experiences. The case study demonstrates how PR can foster a culture of inquiry and continuous improvement within educational institutions, particularly in teacher education

The aim is to give readers a clear understanding of the philosophical foundations of PR and how it differs from traditional research paradigms. The importance of reflection and collaboration in PR to bring about meaningful change is explained, and the case study provides a concrete example of how PR can be implemented in a higher education setting, specifically in the context of teacher education. Those readers wishing to explore PR will find this useful as it describes the cyclical nature of PR, emphasising the importance of action, reflection, and refinement.

In the chapter 'Practitioner Research in Initial Teacher Education' by Vicky Christoforatou, the significance lies in the way it uses a theoretical framework of Stenhouse's Pragmatism to explore the value of the process model in teacher education. It contributes to our understanding of how pre-service teachers, full of curiosity about their new practice, can participate in PR to gain a deeper understanding of their practice. It argues that this is of greater benefit than striving to achieve prescribed curriculum objectives. Readers may consider how this fits with existing initial teacher education and our understanding of the nature of teacher knowledge. This debate is well situated within a wider context of the relationship between practitioner researcher and education policy and thus links well with chapters in Section 3 about the nature of professional learning.

The chapter 'Bridging the Gap: Enhancing Research-Practice Links in Education for a Research-Informed Future' by Adriane Martini examines the fragmented relationship between academic research and educational practices in the UK. Despite the increasing emphasis on evidence-informed practices, a significant gap persists. The text explores initiatives aimed at bridging this divide and potentially improving both practices: research in education and pedagogical choices in the classroom.

The takeaway message is that effective communication channels, the strategic use of technology and knowledge brokers, as well as the ethical commitment to education are essential for fostering a meaningful connection between research and practice. Ultimately, the chapter suggests that a more collaborative and context-sensitive approach can enhance teaching effectiveness and student outcomes in a world increasingly complex and difficult to navigate as educators. Acting as a guide to those facing some of the common problems encountered by practitioner researchers, it makes suggestions for how they might want to develop their work in this field. The text also questions the nature of practitioner research when contrasted with traditional academic research, an area that many newly qualified teachers will be very close to.

Conclusion

We think the chapters chosen reflect PR's sensitivity to context, and its reflective and collaborative character as well as its strong focus on integrating research with the practical realities of teaching.

As well as sharing these common ideas, PR can embrace multiple forms of research, inquiry and practice. These forms can sometimes be in tension. For example, PR can have instrumental goals of improving children's learning and classroom experiences alongside its emancipatory goals. It can test as well as describe and elaborate knowledge, and be, in a sense, 'scientific' as well as practical. It can work through, as well as challenge, existing power structures and school improvement activities. Drawing on and combining theory and evidence, from academic research as well as practice (Perry & Morris, 2023). While it can produce generalisable knowledge, the central goal of PR is the transformation of the educational experiences and outcomes of children.

Rather than viewing these differences and tensions as a problem, we are suggesting that we take a deliberate and systematic approach to recognising various contributions. Practitioner Researchers achieve this through intelligent action and problem solving (Biesta & Burbules, 2003; Dewey, 2008), mastery of professional practices and an understanding of educational and social conditions within their specific contexts (Biesta & Burbules, 2003).

References

Biesta, G. J. J., & Burbules, N. C. (2003). *Pragmatism and educational research*. Rowman & Littlefield.

Dewey, J. (2008). *The later works of John Dewey, volume 12, 1925 – 1953: 1938, Logic: The theory of inquiry* (J. A. Boydston, Ed.). Southern Illinois University Press.

Perry, T., & Morris, R. (2023). *A critical guide to evidence-informed education*. Open University Press.

CHAPTER 1

Practitioner Research in Education: Philosophical Foundations, Contextual Applications, and Policy Implications

Holly Heshmati
University of Warwick, UK

ABSTRACT

This chapter examines practitioner research (PR) in education. PR uniquely positions practitioners and participants at the core of the inquiry, a distinction from research emphasising external observation. Through a case study, the chapter demonstrates the impact of PR in fostering a culture of inquiry in educational settings. The chapter also highlights PR's potential for informing policy decisions by bridging the gap between theory and practice, ensuring policies are grounded in practitioners' and participants' authentic experiences.

Keywords: Practitioner research; educational settings; philosophical foundations; knowledge creation; praxis; teacher resilience

Introduction

Philosophical Foundations of PR

The rise of anti-positivism in the early 20th century led social scientists to embrace new knowledge-building paradigms.

These approaches emphasised the plurality of methods, with validity determined by the specific situation and research questions (Carr, 1994). Practitioner Research (PR) aligns with this perspective, focusing on self-improvement within a professional context to benefit others (Bartlett & Burton, 2006). From this perspective, PR does not necessitate objectivity, but rather acknowledges a socially constructed reality that shapes our daily lives (Brooker & Macpherson, 1999; Tekin & Kotaman, 2013).

While a certain perspective in research views knowledge as an objective, external entity that can be discovered and studied independently of the researcher, PR, on the other hand, recognises that knowledge is socially constructed and influenced by the practitioner's perspective, values, and experiences (Campbell, 2013). In this view, while knowledge may be actively constructed by practitioners, it can still be transferred and shared with others. However, the meaning and relevance of this knowledge may vary depending on the context and the individuals involved. The dynamic nature of knowledge in PR, therefore, highlights the contrast between the traditional view of knowledge as a static entity and the PR perspective that recognises the ongoing evolution and construction of knowledge. That said, most research in the field of social sciences recognise the importance of context in understanding knowledge, however, PR may place a greater emphasis on the role of the practitioner's context and experiences in shaping knowledge as new understandings emerge.

Unlike research focused on identifying universal truths, PR focuses on practical knowledge to enhance the effectiveness of practice (Carr & Kemmis, 2005). This ongoing development is the foundation of PR. At its core, PR challenges the traditional model where research is conducted by academics at a distance from the specific contexts of professional settings. Instead, practitioners themselves become the driving force, investigating questions that emerge directly from their experiences. From this view, practitioner researchers act based on their current understanding, acknowledging its limitations. This aligns with Butler's (1999) view of research as a process of challenging established knowledge structures to explore new possibilities.

This perspective on knowledge claims stems from pragmatism (McNiff, 2013), emphasising the transformation of practice from habit (practice) to informed action (praxis) through critical self-reflection. The aim is to improve social conditions, particularly in educational settings (Campbell, 2013). From this perspective, only critical and emancipatory inquiry constitutes true PR.

While PR being situated within the practitioner's own context ensures its relevance to real-world issues and facilitates positive change (Denscombe, 2010), achieving societal benefits requires personal commitment, seeing things from others' perspectives, and letting go of preconceptions (Oliver, 2014). Therefore, PR begins by addressing problems encountered in practice. The thinking here is that research should not only be used to understand a situation, but to make a positive impact through offering practical solutions to real-world problems. This focus, in educational settings, ensures that research directly addresses the needs of educators, students, and institutions. Moreover, PR's cyclical nature of action, reflection, and refinement fosters continuous improvement. The action-oriented nature of PR makes it highly context-specific, with research grounded in the specific realities of the practitioner's work environment, offering valuable lessons for others facing similar challenges in similar contexts. Rather than seeking generalisation or universal truths, PR focuses on specific realities and tailored solutions.

A Case Study of PR in Higher Education

In this section, to illustrate PR's transformative role in education, I will present a case study from a higher education institution.

As a teacher educator working in an intial teacher training (ITT) institution, my recent focus has been on equipping beginning secondary teachers with the skills, knowledge, and experience necessary to not only survive but thrive in the profession. However, I have become increasingly aware that a lack of resilience can be a major obstacle for these new teachers as they navigate daily challenges. This is particularly concerning given the close link between teacher resilience and teacher retention, which has implications for sustaining quality in the complex and ever-changing school environment (Beltman & Mansfield, 2018).

In exploring potential research approaches, I found PR to be the most suitable for my study because PR as a method enables practitioners to examine their practice systematically, gain insights, and implement changes for improvement (Menter et al., 2011). This approach aligned with my goal of improving my practice through organised research while valuing the knowledge and lived experiences of my participants in a participatory context. Through conducting PR, my aim was to explore strategies that beginning teachers can use to build resilience, potentially improving both their well-being and retention rates. In addition, I was interested in exploring the potential benefits of incorporating a resilience-building programme into teacher education and ITT curricula. Inviting 25 pre-service mathematics teachers to participate in this study, in collaboration with the research participants, I utilised a two-phase design to delve into the experiences of teacher resilience. Phase one explored the participants' perceptions of teacher resilience through qualitative surveys, comparing these to existing literature and research. Based on these findings, resilience-building interventions were developed in collaboration with the participants. In phase two, these interventions were implemented and evaluated using quantitative questionnaires, semi-structured interviews, and observations.

While initial findings suggested prevalent anti-resilient thinking, subsequent data indicated a shift towards recognising the role of supportive environments and personal agency in fostering resilience. In phase one of the research, many participants initially viewed teacher resilience as a personal trait; however, in phase two, after conducting the interventions, the participants gradually developed a more socio-cultural perspective of teacher resilience. From this view, for participants, resilience was no longer solely a product of individual characteristics but was also influenced by the external and internal environments in which teachers work. Findings suggested that teacher resilience was seen as a dynamic, relational construct that developed through interactions between the participants and the context; it was shaped by personal values, dispositions, and the ability to manage various circumstances. Moreover, the study highlighted the importance of cultivating growth-enhancing social resilience in pre-service teacher education and provided implications for developing resilience in ITT.

Conclusion

This participatory research, conducted in collaboration between the researcher and the researched, demonstrated the value of integrating theory and practice, providing multiple benefits. By combining theoretical perspectives with practical insights from the participants, the PR project contributed to a deeper understanding of teacher resilience and its implications for educational practice. In addition, the project's focus on improving educational conditions through research had a positive impact on the ITT institution in which the PR was conducted. Fostering a culture of inquiry and innovation, engagement in this research provided the opportunity for all participants to actively reflect on their experience of teacher resilience and continually experimenting new approaches for building teacher resilience. Creating a dynamic learning environment and ongoing process of reflection and experimentation empowered the participants to identify the most effective strategies to build teacher resilience in pre-service teacher education. In addition, I found the reflective nature of this research helpful in deepening my understanding of my own practice, which promoted continuous learning and professional development. The evidence-based nature of the PR provided data to support educational practices and inform decision-making about ITT curriculum and policies relevant to ITT improvement plans. Finally, the collaboration and knowledge sharing of the PR encouraged me to collaborate and share findings with colleagues, leading to a broader knowledge base. Overall, the research findings suggest that engaging with the PR has the potential to empower both the practitioner and the participants to be reflective and research-engaged individuals who can make informed decisions to improve educational experiences, impacting education policies.

Impact of PR in Educational Settings: A Reflexive Account

In educational settings, PR offers a framework for practitioners to critically examine their own practice in a systematic way, aiming for improvement while building reflection into practice to see relationships between learning and action by explaining what has been learnt (Campbell, 2013). A practitioner researcher should be as reflective about their own teaching as they expect their students to be about their learning. This principle emphasises PR as not merely a methodology, but a philosophy that values the holistic development of the individual. Rooted in the research cycle, PR is a form of reflexive inquiry that practitioners engage in to improve the rationality and justice of their practices, their understanding of these practices, and the contexts in which they occur. Another defining characteristic of PR is participants' collaboration throughout the research design and implementation. This is because achieving social benefits necessitates critical reflection from both researchers and participants, allowing them to identify areas for improvement and build upon existing strengths (Kemmis, 1993). Hence, a key aspect of PR is collaborative reflection which involves making connections between existing and emerging knowledge to create new understandings. By fostering shared understanding of problems and prioritising practical solutions, PR can contribute to addressing educational disparities and promoting inclusive practices and policies.

Response to the Editorial Perspective

The current theoretical understanding of PR in educational settings is multifaceted and evolving. A core aspect, however, is the critique of traditional research perceived as disconnected from the realities of practice, seeking to bridge this gap by allowing practitioners to investigate and develop knowledge directly relevant to their work. In addition, challenging traditional knowledge production models where academics hold exclusive authority over research is another core principle of PR. It emphasises the valuable knowledge embedded within practitioners' experiences and challenges the idea that 'good' research can only come from outside a field by legitimising different forms of knowledge gained through experience and practical problem solving.

This perspective highlights the importance of situated knowledge, the role of power dynamics in research, and the value of marginalised voices – all of which resonate with PR's emphasis on context, reflection, and collaboration. Overall, the theoretical understanding of PR is dynamic and constantly evolving. As the field grows, it is likely to see further development of theoretical frameworks, greater integration with existing research methodologies, and a growing recognition of the valuable contribution practitioners make to knowledge production with frameworks exploring concepts like 'teacher as researcher', and 'communities of practice', all of which emphasise the role of practitioners in knowledge creation.

References

Bartlett, S., & Burton, D. (2006). Practitioner research or descriptions of classroom practice? A discussion of teachers investigating their classrooms. *Educational Action Research*, *14*(3), 395–405.

Beltman, S., & Mansfield, C. F. (2018). Resilience in education: An introduction. In M. Wosnitza, F. Peixoto, S. Beltman, & C.F. Mansfield (Eds.), *Resilience in education: Concepts, contexts and connections* (pp. 3–9). Springer.

Brooker, R., & Macpherson, I. (1999). Communicating the processes and outcomes of practitioner research: An opportunity for self-indulgence or a serious professional responsibility? *Pedagogy, Culture & Society*, *7*(2), 207–221.

Butler, J. (1999). *Gender trouble: Feminist theory and psychoanalytic discourse*. Routledge.

Campbell, K. H. (2013). A call to action: Why we need more practitioner research. A response to "A teacher educator uses action research to develop culturally conscious curriculum planners." *Democracy & Education*, *20*(7), 1–8.

Carr, W. (1994). Whatever happened to action research? *Educational Action Research*, *2*(3), 427–436.

Carr, W., & Kemmis, S. (2005). Staying critical. *Educational Action Research*, *13*(3), 347–358.

Denscombe, M. (2010). *The good research guide for small scale research projects* (4th ed.). Open University Press.

Kemmis, S. (1993). Action research and social movement: A challenge for policy research. *Education Policy Analysis Archives, 1*(1), 1–8. https://digitalcommons.usf.edu/usf_EPAA/251

McNiff, J. (2013). *Action research: Principles and practice* (3rd ed.). Routledge.

Menter, I., Elliot, D., Hulme, M., Lewin, J., & Lowden, K. (2011). *A guide to practitioner research in education*. SAGE.

Oliver, P. (2014). The conclusion. In *Writing your thesis* [online]. SAGE (pp. 181–191). https://doi.org/10.4135/9781446294994.n12

Tekin, A. K., & Kotaman, H. (2013). The epistemological perspectives on action research. *Journal of Educational and Social Research, 3*(1), 81–91. https://doi.org/10.5901/jesr.2013.v3n1p81

CHAPTER 2

Practitioner Research in Initial Teacher Education

Vicky Christoforatou
University of East Anglia, UK

ABSTRACT

Initial Teacher Training (ITT) providers are required to adhere to statutory guidance that determines content, structure, assessment, and the management of training programmes (DfE, 2022). Added to this, the ITT curriculum is pre-defined in a core curriculum mandated by the government (DfE, 2019a). Stenhouse (1975) argued for a 'process' rather than an 'objectives' curriculum model that defines learning not as a target to be hit but something to be deepened in the context of Humanities teaching. The objectives model now underpins the domain of teachers' professional learning and training, especially since the introduction of the core curriculum. An objectives model in ITT presumes a technical model of teaching and requires pre-service teachers to demonstrate certain behaviours. This chapter explores the value of the process model in teacher education where pre-service teachers participate in practitioner research to gain a deeper understanding of their practice, rather than to achieve prescribed curriculum objectives. In this process, pre-service teachers are viewed as both producers and consumers of knowledge.

Keywords: Teacher training; teacher researcher; mentoring; objectives model; process model

Introduction

In my current role as teacher educator, I work with English trainee teachers on the year-long Secondary Postgraduate

Certificate of Education (PGCE) course at the University of East Anglia, which combines university-based training and two school placement experiences. Throughout the course, trainees demonstrate genuine curiosity about teaching English and ask questions such as *how can I help pupils to generate ideas for creative writing?*; or *why pupils find it difficult to analyse the structure of texts?* This disposition towards inquiry often corresponds to other qualities such as passion for the subject, commitment to working with young people and continuous self-reflection. Cochran-Smith and Lytle (2009) refer to this kind of inquiry as 'stance' to suggest a way of knowing and working in classrooms that invites critical questioning and systematic research. I would, therefore, argue that trainee teachers, at the beginning of their training journey, have the mindset of Stenhouse's *teacher as researcher*. Stenhouse defined educational research as 'systematic and sustained inquiry, planned and self-critical' (1981, p. 113). As teacher researchers, trainee teachers can make hypotheses about their own practice and test these in their classrooms to develop pedagogical knowledge. I suggest that teacher education should foster trainee teachers' engagement with educational research and develop their professional identity as practitioner researchers. This chapter explores some of the benefits as well as obstacles in adopting Stenhouse's model in Initial Teacher Education in England.

Discussion

The Benefits of Practitioner Research in Initial Teacher Education

The first benefit is teacher development. All teachers are continuously developing their knowledge and understanding of pupils, didactics, and teaching materials. It is worth quoting Stenhouse in full:

> *Teachers must be educated to develop their art, not to master it, for the claim to mastery merely signals the abandoning of aspiration. Teaching is not to be regarded as a static accomplishment like riding a bicycle*

or keeping a ledger; it is, like all acts of high ambition, a strategy in the face of an impossible task. (1979, p. 131)

If *teachers must be educated* (my emphasis) to develop the art of teaching, then asking systematic questions about and reflecting on their practice is an authentic professional exercise that should be embedded in teacher education programmes. Mentors and educators (*like me*) may feel justified to give trainees the 'recipes' on how to be successful in the classroom, but care is needed to avoid rendering trainees dependent on these recipes, undermining the potential for future growth and aspiration. Practitioner research sees teachers as producers and not only consumers of knowledge who ask their own questions about their teaching.

Another benefit of practitioner research in ITT relates to the nature of teacher knowledge. In practitioner research, knowledge is not generated exclusively outside the domain of practice nor is it the privilege of experts. Equally, the direction of theory/practice does not necessarily need to be one-directional; both classroom experience and university learning can generate theory. There is an underlying assumption that theoretical knowledge is a commodity, produced in a university and then given to trainee teachers to implement in placement. In practitioner research, knowledge about teaching is context-specific, linking theory and practice organically through practitioner research. Elliott refers to this as a 're-contextualized conception of educational theory – one that is fused with the concept of phronesis' that 'may help teachers to reclaim their activities as having a space for praxis' (2013, p. 32). Practitioner research in ITT positions trainees on the same learning journey as other teachers investigating new links between the university curriculum and placement practice, as well as testing these new links in fresh contexts and with different classes, topics, and pupil groups.

The Obstacles of Practitioner Research in Initial Teacher Education

The main obstacle lies in the uncomfortable relationship between practitioner research and education policy. One recent example is the introduction of the Core Content Framework (CCF, DfE, 2019) mandating the minimum content of the ITT curriculum for all trainee teachers across phases and specialisms. The CCF specifies curriculum objectives in 'Learn That' and 'Learn How To' statements that trainee teachers are required to know. This marked a clear policy shift to an objectives model of the ITT curriculum: a prescribed curriculum to be learned, rehearsed and applied in the classroom. In order for pre-service teachers to be researchers, the curriculum cannot predominantly consist of statements to be learned.

Stenhouse (1975) argued for a 'process' rather than an 'objectives' curriculum model that defines learning not as a target to be hit but something to be deepened. The values of inquiry are intrinsic qualities in the discipline of teacher education which concerns itself with *why*: 'An objectives-based curriculum is like a site-plan simplified so that people know exactly where to dig their trenches without having to know why' (Stenhouse, 1985, p. 85). The objectives model now underpins the domain of teachers' professional learning and training, especially since the introduction of the CCF. The curriculum objectives in the CCF presume a technical model of teaching expressed in targets and behaviours. The premise is that teacher knowledge can be complete, which distorts the nature of knowledge in ITT; teacher knowledge is always developing. On the other hand, the 'process model' would allow trainee teachers to develop a deeper understanding of their practice, rather than meeting prescribed curriculum objectives. This does not signify that ITT curriculum objectives should be scrapped but rather treated as processes recognising the complexity of teaching. However, it does mean that infusing the curriculum with the 'process model' must be a condition for trainees' participation in practitioner research; otherwise, there is no space for authentic questions about the real problems trainees' face in the classroom as they acculturate to a professional identity of inquiry.

A further obstacle is the distinction between expert/novice in the roles of mentor/educator and trainee teacher. In the CCF, 'expert colleagues' involved in the trainees' development include 'professional colleagues, experienced and effective teachers, subject specialists, mentors, lecturers and tutors' (CCF, 2019a).

The remainder of the document elaborates on the kinds of mentoring activity that these *experts* will undertake so that trainees can demonstrate the 'how to' requirements. The conflict with practitioner research lies in the expertise of the mentor that trainee teachers are required to emulate in their practice. As Noffke points out,

> *the idea of beginning and experienced teachers working together in inquiry communities talks back to the current emphasis on teacher 'expertise,' which implies certainty and state-of-the-art practice while the novice is one who learns effective practices by imitating the strategies of his or her more competent colleagues.* (2009, p. 46)

The *certainty* of the expert and *imitative* behaviour expected of the trainee hinders practitioner research.

Finally, the issue of performativity. The government agenda in England with 'the intervention of successive governments for more than a quarter of a century, has resulted in increased levels of regulation, a focus on performativity and regular compliance monitoring' (Tatto et al., 2017, p. 241). Similarly, Goodwyn comments that the Teachers' Standards 'may be characterised as still essentially a competence model with slightly more emphasis on performativity' (2012, p. 42). I would suggest here that the application of a process or an objectives model in teacher education encompasses these concerns about the competence model in ITT and quantifying teacher learning. An objectives model in ITT is rather policy-friendly: curriculum objectives are identified; teacher training is regulated, and performance is assessed against set criteria. Then, policy makers can claim success as the objectives have been met, the ITT curriculum learned, and the quality of training provision deemed good (mainly because it was consistent across different contexts/disciplines/phases).

Conclusion

All ITT stakeholders, including the policy makers, educators, and mentors, want to develop good teachers. If we agreed that 'good teachers are necessarily autonomous in professional judgement' (Stenhouse, 1985, p. 104), then we could start to acknowledge that a process model in ITT is a condition for trainees' engagement with practitioner research. This would allow the space for trainee teachers to cultivate autonomy in learning how to identify and articulate problems; ask systematic and authentic questions; and see themselves as agents in the production of pedagogical knowledge. Perhaps, this might alleviate the recruitment and retention issue (DfE, 2019b) in England and support trainee teachers to thrive and be happy in their classrooms. Instead of focusing on solving the symptoms such as teacher workload and well-being, policy should focus on recognising trainee teachers' professional autonomy and judgement.

Response to the Editorial Perspective

As outlined in the editorial perspective of this volume, one of the aims and responsibilities of the Practitioner Research SIG includes 'fostering research skills and research knowledge' and 'supporting colleagues to become critical and reflective in their practice and/or research'. Including trainee teachers in these aims is equally important as it would facilitate their engagement with research throughout their careers. In my previous role, I had worked as a secondary English teacher for 20 years and my relationship with research was somewhat disaffected. It was not until I became a teacher educator and enrolled on a doctorate programme that I began to see myself as a researcher. Looking back in my own training and early career, I clearly did not have the tools, access to educational research and resources to be engaged with research. In 'What training do teachers need?', Orchard and Winch argue that beginning teachers must engage with empirical educational research and be taught 'how research works and how to be researchers' (2015, p. 23). In other words, doing research and learning how to think in practice needs to be in the ITT curriculum. At the same time, academic researchers and Higher Education Institutions also have a significant role to play in facilitating practitioner research during the training years and beyond (for example, Elliott & Christoforatou, 2024). Otherwise, teachers (like my earlier self) will continue to be othered by research.

References

Cochran-Smith, M., & Lytle, S. L. (2009). *Inquiry as stance: Practitioner research for the next generation*. Teachers College Press.

Department for Education (DfE). (2019a). *ITT Core Content Framework*. https://assets.publishing.service.gov.uk/government/uploads/system/uploads/attachment_data/file/974307/ITT_core_content_framework_.pdf

Department for Education (DfE). (2019b). *Teacher recruitment and retention strategy*. https://www.gov.uk/government/publications/teacher-recruitment-and-retention-strategy

Department for Education (DfE). (2022). *Initial teacher training (ITT): Criteria and supporting advice*. https://www.gov.uk/government/publications/initial-teacher-training-criteria/initial-teacher-training-itt-criteria-and-supporting-advice

Elliott, J. (2013). Professional education and the idea of a practical educational science. In J. Elliott (Ed.), Reconstructing teacher education (pp. 45–63). Routledge.

Elliott, J., & Christoforatou, V. (Eds.). (2024). *Linking theory with practice in the classroom: A hybrid model of lesson study research in action* (1st ed.). Routledge.

Goodwyn, A. (2012). One size fits all: The increasing standardisation of English teachers' work in England. *English Teaching: Practice & Critique (University of Waikato)*, 11(4), 36–53.

Noffke, S. (2009). Revisiting the professional, personal, and political dimensions of action research. In B. Somekh, & S. Noffke (Eds.), *The SAGE handbook of educational action research* (pp. 6–24). Sage Publications.

Orchard, J., & Winch, C. (2015). What training do teachers need? Why theory is necessary to good teaching. In *Impact philosophical perspectives on education policy* (Vol. 22, pp. 1–39). Wiley Blackwell.

Stenhouse, L. (1975). *An introduction to curriculum research and development*. Heinemann.

Stenhouse, L. (1979). Research basis for as a teaching. In J. Elliott & N. Norris (Eds.), *Curriculum, pedagogy and educational research: The work of Lawrence Stenhouse* (pp. 122–137). Taylor & Francis Group, Florence.

Stenhouse, L. (1981). What counts as research? *British Journal of Educational Studies*, 29(2), 103–114.

Stenhouse, L. (1985). Research as a basis for teaching: readings from the work of Lawrence Stenhouse. In J. Rudduck & D. Hopkins

(Eds.), *Research as a basis for teaching: Readings from the work of Lawrence Stenhouse*. Heinemann Educational Books.

Tatto, M. T., Burn, K., Menter, I., Mutton, T., & Thompson, I. (2017). *Learning to teach in England and the United States: The evolution of policy and practice* (1st ed.). Routledge.

CHAPTER 3

Bridging the Gap: Enhancing Research-Practice Links in Education for a Research-Informed Future

Adriane Martini
University College School, UK

ABSTRACT

This chapter examines the fragmented relationship between academic research and educational practices in England. Despite the increasing emphasis on evidence-informed practices, a significant gap persists. The chapter explores initiatives aimed at bridging this divide. It argues that effective communication channels, the strategic use of technology and knowledge broker, as well as the ethical commitment to education, are essential for fostering a meaningful connection between research and practice. Ultimately, the chapter suggests that a more collaborative and context-sensitive approach can enhance teaching effectiveness and student outcomes in a world increasingly complex and difficult to navigate as educators.

Keywords: Research-informed practices; evidence-informed practices; educational research; knowledge brokers; affinity spaces; professional learning networks; professional development

Introduction

Education in England has increasingly shifted towards research-informed practices over the past few decades, gaining momentum in the 2010s. Evidence of this move can be seen via a few important developments in the education research landscape. The establishment of the Education Endowment Foundation (EEF) in 2011 marked a significant move towards evidence-based interventions. Similarly, the Chartered College of Teaching was created in 2017, focusing on accrediting teachers who complete their training in evidence-informed practices. In 2016, the Department for Education emphasised that effective 'professional development should be underpinned by robust evidence and expertise' (DfE, 2016, p. 6). The Office for Standards in Education, Children's Services and Skills (Ofsted) has increasingly stressed the importance of research-informed practices in its inspection frameworks, stating that their judgements are guided by '(...) our inspection experience, areas of consensus in *academic research* and our *own research*' (Ofsted, 2024). Multiple and diverse online initiatives followed in an attempt to offer relatable and easy to digest content. Despite these efforts, bridging the gap between research and practice remains challenging (Cochran et al., 1993; Shulman, 1987). What is the shift reflecting and why should we bridge the gap between academic research and everyday classroom practices?

Discussion

The debate surrounding the state of education often begins with the proposition that the educational system as a whole needs 'radical improvements' (Ashton, 1996), or a 'radical transformation' (Robinson, 2017). When discussing teacher education, this argument arises partly due to a perceived failure of training programmes to effectively close the gap between theory and practical implementation beyond the initial training phase (Korthagen et al., 2006), culminating in a 'reality shock' (Veenman, 1984) whereby teachers are confronted with a complexity of factors in every-day education that cannot be resolved by the direct application of knowledge acquired in training.

It all makes sense if we stop for a second to consider the current societal changes and technological advances that are, undoubtedly, affecting what education should be like. Teachers are expected to, somehow, keep up with the complex and sophisticated developments in cognitive neuroscience and all it has contributed to understanding how people learn (Howard-Jones, 2014). Parallel to that, schools are facing pressures to cope with an unprecedented mental health crisis among young people, not to mention the need to adapt to emerging narratives around intersectionality, representation and decolonisation of ideas. Add to that the challenges posed by the recent revolution (or threat) of Artificial Intelligence (AI) promises in the contemporary educational context (Selwyn, 2019).

It is no surprise that teachers remain sceptical about the benefits of engaging with the slow pace of academic research. For example, Early Career Teachers (ECT) are 'much less likely to indicate their needs were met by professional associations, books and journals and professional development beyond their own schools' (Carpenter et al., 2022, p. 801), and mention social media and websites as their most common source of professional learning (Spencer et al., 2018). This seems to suggest that teachers are looking for alternatives to traditional approaches to professional development (PD), frequently described as 'one-size-fits-all set of solutions that often fail to distinguish between the needs of different teachers' (Hofman & Dijkstra, 2010).

Bridging the Gap Between Academic Research and Classroom Practices

However, the demand for reliable insights into education remains strong as teachers recognise its constantly evolving nature. Connecting with current research offers tangible benefits, such as improved students' academic performance and wellbeing. Educators also gain by staying informed about the latest pedagogical advancements and refining their teaching methods. This ongoing learning process not only enhances job satisfaction but also supports teacher retention.

In today's complex and everchanging world, creating a culture of innovation and openness to change is key to integrating research into schools. Next, I offer three ideas that could support this process.

The Three Possible Directions

Redefining Practitioner Research's Identity

This is perhaps the most personal part of the chapter, rooted in my reflections as a practitioner-researcher. Having recently completed an MSc in Teacher Education while working as a secondary school teacher, I often found the connections between academic research and classroom practice tenuous.

Due to my mixed academic background, I aimed to engage in the dialogue between Philosophy and the Sciences in my research – something Psychology, in my view, does well. However, I was often reminded that my work should not align strictly with either field and should remain somewhere in between. This left me uncertain about the scope and methods of educational research, and I was, quite frankly, unimpressed by much of the academic work in this area. With few exceptions, most papers I reviewed over the past two years concluded with vague statements like, 'more research is needed' or 'this topic is too complex', offering little impact beyond a specialised audience.

This contrasts sharply with the more impactful contributions from other fields, such as Paulo Freire's work in Philosophy of Education or ground-breaking theories in Cognitive Psychology. It raises important questions: Is educational research facing an identity crisis? Should we better define its methodologies, or give educators more freedom to use the tools they deem appropriate for their inquiries? The latter seems more appealing but would require a shift in how we approach research. To embrace academic freedom, we must accept that valuable research can occur beyond university walls – free from bureaucracy, rigid hierarchies, and detachment from the traditional academic model of research.

However, to be taken seriously, such research must still draw from philosophical and scientific methods that allow for systematic, rigorous exploration. The survival and relevance of educational research depend on this balance. If we want teachers to value research throughout their careers, staying relevant and inspirational must remain the goal.

Professional Learning Networks (PLNs) and the Knowledge Broker

PLNs are groups of professionals who collaborate beyond their own contexts to improve the quality of their work (Brown & Poortman, 2018). PLNs are grounded in collaboration, purpose, and reflective professional inquiry (Yancovic et al., 2019), and are composed of professionals actively engaged in education.

One challenge is that day-to-day practitioners need to be available and willing to participate in research development. This is where knowledge or research brokers can make a difference. Brokers are 'network members who occupy key structural positions to link networks with their own institution' (Yancovic et al., 2019, p. 4). They facilitate knowledge transfer, sharing, and use between researchers and practitioners, playing a critical role in bridging the gap between evidence and practice, especially in education (Phipps & Morton, 2013). Knowledge brokers identify relevant research, synthesise evidence, translate findings into practical applications, and facilitate communication between researchers and practitioners. Brown and Flood (2019) argue that school leadership plays a key role in creating and supporting knowledge brokers by prioritising PLNs and positioning brokers as their representatives.

However, challenges exist. From my perspective as someone with a job title akin to a knowledge broker, I am acutely aware this is rare in state-funded schools. Resource constraints are a significant barrier, as funding and institutional support are critical for sustaining these roles.

Nevertheless, research shows that knowledge brokers can improve pedagogical practices by ensuring practitioners have access to the best available evidence (Chapman & Muijs, 2014). They foster collaboration between researchers and practitioners, leading to more relevant research. Knowledge brokers also distil the overwhelming volume of content into actionable insights, making research more accessible to educators immersed in the demands of teaching.

New Technologies and Social Media

Social media and new technologies, such as AI, are filling a gap that traditional PD cannot. Their flexibility, diversity, personalisation, and accessibility make them appealing. For instance, up to December 2022, the platform X had nearly 368 million active users, and Facebook remains the most popular with 3.07 billion users (Statista, 2025). These platforms offer access to diverse professional communities that can cater to niche interests.

Gee (2005) introduced the term 'affinity spaces', where people affiliate based on shared activities, interests, or goals. Given the context-dependent nature of education, allowing professionals to find relevant information and PD represents a significant improvement in applying research to practise. In affinity spaces, knowledge is co-constructed by decentralised networks of individuals (Carpenter et al., 2022). In today's world, creating spaces where diversity not only coexists but contributes to the development of ideas in education is essential.

Social media also disseminates research to a broad audience, benefiting professionals in remote or politically restricted areas, making knowledge more accessible and equitable. It is no surprise that organisations like the EEF and the Chartered College of Teaching use social media to share research projects, alongside popular accounts like Edutopia and Teacher Toolkit.

However, social media has its critics. For example, X's character limit may restrict deep discussions, leading to oversimplification of research. Instagram's focus on visual content may not suit complex educational topics. Additionally, the lack of peer review on social media makes it difficult to ensure the quality of shared research. Educators must curate their feeds, which limits the advantages to those who are tech-savvy or well-connected (Carpenter et al., 2022).

Conclusion

A principle that is widely discussed is that education has a layer of ethical engagement, based on fostering positive relationships grounded in empathy, respect, and a sense of responsibility towards one another (Freire, 1967). Loughran (2005) proposes an affiliated idea in arguing that 'the heart and soul of teaching begins with relationships' (p. 86) and that these relationships should be characterised by sensitivity towards each other's needs, building trust between teachers and learners, being honest without fearing being vulnerable and valuing independence rather than hierarchical structures. Education should be a process grounded on the ability of an individual to critically think about the world and transform it; this must be at the core of how we think about this education for the future. Whilst this idea might sound too idealistic to fit in the discussion developed thus far, I believe that returning to the core values of what education should be for is at the heart of maintaining the connection between the every-day job and the efforts to continue the research on how young people can thrive. Either that, or there is little motivation for teachers to value what research can bring to their practices.

References

Ashton, P. T. (1996). Improving the preparation of teachers. *Educational Researcher*, 25(9), 21–35.

Brown, C., & Flood, J. (2019). *Formalise, prioritise and mobilise: How school leaders secure the benefits of professional learning networks*. Emerald Publishing Limited.

Brown, C., & Poortman, C. L. (Eds.). (2018). *Networks for learning: Effective collaboration for teacher, school and system improvement*. Routledge, Taylor & Francis Group.

Carpenter, J., Tani, T., Morrison, S., & Keane, J. (2022). Exploring the landscape of educator professional activity on Twitter. *Professional Development in Education*, 48(5), 784–805.

Chapman, C., & Muijs, D. (2014). Does school-to-school collaboration promote school improvement? A study of the impact of school federations on student outcomes. *School Effectiveness and School Improvement*, 25(3), 351–393.

Cochran, K. F., DeRuiter, J. A., & King, R. A. (1993). Pedagogical content knowing: An integrative model for teacher preparation. *Journal of Teacher Education*, 44(4), 263–272.

DfE. (2016, July). *Standard for teachers' professional development: Implementation guidance for school leaders, teachers, and organisations that offer professional development for teachers*. DfE.

Freire, P. (1967). *Educação como prática da liberdade*. Paz e Terra.

Gee, J. P. (2005). Semiotic social spaces and affinity spaces: From *The Age of Mythology* to today's schools. In D. Barton & K. Tusting (Eds.), *Beyond communities of practice* (1st ed., pp. 214–232). Cambridge University Press.

Hofman, R. H., & Dijkstra, B. J. (2010). Effective teacher professionalization in networks? *Teaching and Teacher Education*, 26(4), 1031–1040.

Howard-Jones, P. A. (2014). Neuroscience and education: Myths and messages. *Nature Reviews Neuroscience*, 15(12), 817–824.

Korthagen, F., Loughran, J., & Russell, T. (2006). Developing fundamental principles for teacher education programs and practices. *Teaching and Teacher Education*, 22(8), 1020–1041.

Loughran, J. (2005). *Developing a pedagogy of teacher education understanding teaching & learning about teaching*. Taylor and Francis.

Ofsted. (2024, April 5). *School inspection handbook*. https://www.gov.uk/government/publications/school-inspection-handbook-eif/school-inspection-handbook-for-september-2023

Phipps, D., & Morton, S. (2013). Qualities of knowledge brokers: Reflections from practice. *Evidence & Policy*, 9(2), 255–265.

Robinson, K. (2017). *Out of our minds: The power of being creative* (3rd ed.). CAPSTONE.

Selwyn, N. (2019). *Should robots replace teachers? AI and the future of education*. Polity Press.

Shulman, L. S. (1987). Knowledge and teaching: Foundations of the new reform. *Harvard Educational Review*, 57(1), 1–23.

Spencer, P., Harrop, S., Thomas, J., & Cain, T. (2018). The professional development needs of early career teachers, and the extent to which they are met: A survey of teachers in England. *Professional Development in Education*, 44(1), 33–46.

Statista. (2025). *Most popular social networks worldwide as of January 2025, ranked by number of monthly active users*. Retrieved on October 2, 2025 from https://www.statista.com/statistics/272014/global-social-networks-ranked-by-number-of-users/

Veenman, S. (1984). Perceived problems of beginning teachers. *Review of Educational Research*, 54(2), 143–178.

Yancovic, M. P., Torres, A. G., Figueroa, L. A., & Chapman, C. (2019). *School improvement networks and collaborative inquiry: Fostering systematic change in challenging contexts*. Emerald Publishing Limited.

Introduction to Section 2: Power, Positionality, and Identity in Practitioner Research

Kate Mawson
Nottingham Trent University, UK

In contemporary education, practitioner research increasingly demands that educators grapple with questions of identity, positionality, and power. As teachers step into the dual role of practitioner and researcher, they find themselves moving between spaces – simultaneously insiders and critical observers of their own practice. This shifting identity offers unique opportunities for deeper engagement, authentic inquiry, and transformative professional development, but it also brings challenges that require careful negotiation. Section 2 explores how practitioner-researchers navigate these tensions, highlighting how insider status, intersectionality, and reflexivity shape both research processes and outcomes.

Throughout these chapters, a common thread emerges: the practitioner-researcher is not a neutral presence. Rather, their lived experiences, professional histories, and social identities deeply influence how they interact with participants, construct knowledge, and challenge power dynamics. Rebekah Gear and Tazreen Kassim-Lowe reflect on this complexity, offering insights into the 'in-between' space occupied by those who straddle education and research. Their chapter explores how recursive, evolving identities affect belonging and credibility in both fields. They show that embracing this fluid identity is not a weakness but a powerful stance – one that can foster more meaningful engagement with both peers and the communities they serve.

The notion that insider research can transform not just individual practice but broader professional cultures is also developed by Dr Rachel Marsden and Dr Gillian Peiser. Their exploration of empowering teachers as research-engaged professionals demonstrates how practitioner research challenges traditional hierarchies and repositions teachers as knowledge creators. They argue that when educators are given the tools and autonomy to critically engage with research, they disrupt institutional norms, creating more participatory and democratic educational spaces.

However, being an insider also presents ethical and relational complexities, particularly when working within familiar workplace environments. Dr Sarah Peters and Dr Joyce I-Hui Chen examine these tensions, showing how FE practitioners must navigate existing structures of authority while pursuing research intended to improve practice. Their chapter offers a real-world account of how practitioner-researchers negotiate positionality and manage power dynamics to ensure that their work remains ethical, inclusive, and impactful. They highlight the importance of critically reflecting on one's own position to mitigate risks and maximise the transformative potential of insider research.

At the same time, new methodological approaches offer practitioner-researchers tools for reimagining their roles and relationships with participants. Dr Frances-Ann Norton's chapter highlights an arts-based research method piloted across three European universities, showing how creative practices can open up new spaces for reflection and dialogue. By using arts-based approaches, practitioner-researchers can transcend traditional research boundaries, inviting participants to engage with complex issues of identity and power in more accessible and emotionally resonant ways.

Finally, Sylvia Ikomi's deeply personal reflection on delivering CPD sessions around the adultification of Black girls offers a powerful example of how identity and intersectionality can shape practitioner research. Ikomi shows that shared identity between researcher and participants can foster a profound sense of belonging, enhancing both trust and knowledge exchange. Her chapter underscores the importance of recognising and valuing lived experience within practitioner research, especially when addressing systemic inequalities and promoting social justice.

Together, these chapters reveal that practitioner research is inherently relational, political, and personal. Navigating the spaces between practice and research requires reflexivity, courage, and a willingness to confront the ways power and identity shape every aspect of the work. Far from being a simple extension of teaching, practitioner research emerges here as a transformative endeavour – one that empowers educators not only to improve their own practice but also to challenge structures of inequality and foster more inclusive educational environments.

By embracing their unique positions as insiders, while remaining critically aware of the complexities this brings, practitioner-researchers create new possibilities for change, belonging, and collective growth in education.

CHAPTER 4

Empowering a Research-Engaged Profession

Rachel Marsden[a] and Gillian Peiser[b]
[a]Edge Hill University, UK
[b]Liverpool John Moores University, UK

ABSTRACT

This chapter presents three examples of practitioner research (PR) in different school contexts in England. The authors have been playful with the term PR engagement, using here the term 'engaging *with* research' for practitioners who critique existing research, and 'engaging *in* research' for practitioners conducting their own research. As well as more traditional modes of research engagement, a more inclusive research practice is presented here: '*re-searching*' one's own practice through reflective activities (Marsden, 2020).

Keywords: Research engagement; reflective practice; continuing professional development; senior leadership; professionalism; agency

Introduction

Recent policy rhetoric in England has positioned teaching as an 'evidence-informed *profession*' (emphasis added) (DfE, March 2016, p. 37). According to Evetts (2013), what differentiates a profession from an occupation is the agency to contribute to a shared knowledge base. PR, involving various modes of research engagement, offers possibilities for this grassroots construction of knowledge, which Carr and Kemmis (1986/2002) conceptualised as educational enlightenment. Carr and Kemmis' (1986/2002) notion of the enlightened critical teacher is of one who may reflect on existing research, or one's own practice, but ideally generate their own findings to interrogate the knowledge base generated by external others.

This chapter presents three vignettes of different forms of PR. They have been constructed from qualitative data from interviews conducted during Marsden's (2020) doctoral study, which received the appropriate ethical approval. It is hoped that they will provide ideas for senior leaders to empower a research-engaged profession. Developing Goswami and Stillman's (1987, p. 30) concept of teacher researchers 'looking – and looking again', we postulate that '*re*-searching' (quite literally, 'looking again' at one's practice) is a good starting point for PR.

Discussion

Vignettes of PR Engagement

To preserve anonymity, pseudonyms are used, reminiscent of social media handles (Goodyear et al., 2019), indicating participants' position in their school. Each practitioner researcher revealed specific aspects of their identity, power, and positionality, with each of these elements influencing the teacher's research practices in different ways.

@MrSEND: Identifying as a *Re*-searcher

In a secondary school for young people with special educational needs and disabilities (SEND), it was decided that continuing professional development (CPD) for an academic year would take the form of individual research projects for all teachers and Teaching Assistants (TAs). Each practitioner was to focus upon a particular student and research ways to help that individual. This involved careful reflection and attention to students' individual education plans (IEPs). In effect, staff were to *re*-search their current practice, i.e. to look again at their craft. This CPD activity took place during dedicated non-teaching time to avoid any extra burden. In this allotted time, staff were to devise certain strategies and then reflect upon their implementation. Colleagues then disseminated their findings to one another via presentations to learn from each other.

A middle leader in the school, @MrSEND, believed that he was empowered to construct a knowledge base that was more relevant to his unique context. This was preferable to basing his practice on someone else's academic research, which is arguably a more passive process (see Godfrey & Brown, 2018). Furthermore, in his view, outputs constructed by teachers were more accessible to busy practitioners, who do not have time to read long academic publications. He was glad that he was not expected to write a research report on his findings, presenting, instead, in a mode more familiar to teachers.

One might argue that the nature of research in this school represented typical CPD and did not differ to what teachers do all the time. After all, the Teachers' Standards in England mandate that teachers 'reflect systematically on the effectiveness of lessons and approaches to teaching' (DfE, 2011, p. 11). However, such reflection may be an introspective activity. In contrast, the practitioners in this school were empowered to work collaboratively in developing a shared knowledge base that is useable by others in their unique context. This kind of grassroots CPD is not promoted by the Department for Education's (July 2016) Standard for Professional Development, which positions teachers as passive recipients of evidence gathered by external researchers. @MrSEND identified himself as a researcher because, together with his colleagues, he was an active agent in constructing and disseminating knowledge. These critical reflections are part of what Winch et al. (2013) identified as professional knowledge, along with tacit and technical knowledge. We argue that the hyphenated term '*re*-searcher' more accurately highlights the active process of searching one's own practice to address localised issues, which may act as a springboard for future engagement *with* research more broadly.

@MsDeputy: Empowering Staff to Engage *with* Research

In a primary school that had recently been designated as a Research School (RSN, n.d.), a senior leader, @MsDeputy, organised research seminars for staff within the Academy Trust. @MsDeputy valued the research of academics and when interviewed, expressed her pride about her membership of the British Educational Research Association (BERA). She had attended BERA's annual conference, paid for by the school, so she could network with established researchers and invite them to present their research findings to the Academy Trust practitioners. The invited speakers were to give presentations in voluntary CPD seminars after school. To persuade researchers to participate, @MsDeputy offered to publicise their future projects to facilitate the recruitment of research participants. @MsDeputy also said she was aware that academics were encouraged to disseminate their findings beyond academia, and the CPD seminars provided them with a platform for doing so. In this way, practitioners were able to access the latest research, making the initiative mutually beneficial.

The goal was to empower practitioners to interrogate the research presented by academics, drawing on experiences from their own practice to challenge the findings in a dialogic way (Wall & Hall, 2017). @MsDeputy disclosed, however, that she was disappointed that after a year of half-termly seminars, the intended collaborative exchange of knowledge was still a 'work in progress'. Delegates at the seminars did not question the researchers, perhaps because they lacked confidence or prior experience of critical engagement with research. Although the researchers were outsiders entering the physical space of the school, perhaps the normative identity of 'researcher' was seen to overpower the professional identity of the 'practitioner'. Therefore, although practitioners were provided with the opportunity to engage critically with research, the power dynamic created by the format meant that this was not fulfilled.

Nonetheless, practitioners were provided with access to current thinking, which, according to Hordern (2016), is important for a profession. Knowledge from research is often behind a 'paywall' or only accessible by enrolling on higher education (HE) courses (Maxwell et al., 2015). In this context, there was, nevertheless, still a cost to this research engagement since the school funded the seminars from their Research Schools

Network budget. Whilst not all schools will be able to do this, teachers can connect with their local Research School to partake in opportunities like this, as recommended in a report by the Royal Society & British Academy (2018). Without it being part of the CPD allocation for practitioners, though, voluntary initiatives like this run the risk of excluding those who have other commitments beyond their work. The ideal would be to empower all teachers to engage with research by normalising this as part of dedicated CPD time.

@MrIndependent: Positionality as a Teacher Engaging in Research

In a fee-paying school that partly funded Master's courses for staff, one middle leader, @MrIndependent, relished in engaging in his own research project. @MrIndependent considered himself as a 'natural academic' and thought that his aptitude for discovery had motivated him. Reflecting on the matter that one must have the means as well as the inclination, he realised that it was only now, near the end of his career, that he was able to contribute to the fees as he no longer had significant financial or family commitments. He admitted that partaking in a Master's degree at the later stage of his career meant that he might not be able to embed his findings in his practice. Nevertheless, @MrIndependent found the process of researching to be beneficial, and he thought that he and his pupils benefited from his research engagement in other tangential ways.

@MrIndependent's identity as a teacher morphed, not only into a researcher, but also a learner. This identity shift afforded him more empathy with his pupils; he re-positioned himself as a role model for his pupils to see the value of life-long learning. In staff meetings also, he felt that he had more 'clout', as he was able to point to research to support his contributions in what Foreman-Peck and Heilbronn (2018) have argued is a democratising function of PR. @MrIndependent, therefore, was empowered by his access to research through his HE course, and re-positioned himself as both a source of authority amongst colleagues, and an empathetic teacher to his students. He repeated the necessity for practitioners to be funded to engage in HE courses like he was. Funding earlier on in one's career would transform practitioners into practitioner researchers who are able to contribute to the knowledge base that will inform their practice, and that of others.

Enabling teachers to engage in research in this way, however, does not overcome the other barrier that @MrIndpendent had encountered in the early days of his career: time constraints. In order for research engagement to have a positive impact on practitioners earlier in their careers, and to elevate teacher agency and professionalism, research engagement should be integrated into school CPD as a normative practice (Royal Society & British Academy, 2018).

Conclusion

As these vignettes illustrate, PR can encompass a range of activities that can empower teachers, as in Carr and Kemmis' (1986/2002) conceptual framework. If PR is to be enacted in the teaching profession, however, endorsement and prioritisation from school leaders is necessary (Brown et al., 2018). We have seen how PR may be funded from the school's budget, whether that is to pay for conference attendance, or to partially fund a Master's degree. These models could be cost-effective, according to Thomas (2017), as an alternative to one-off CPD sessions delivered by a consultant in which practitioners are passive recipients of knowledge.

A less costly model of research engagement as CPD has been to build what we identify as '*re*-search' into the workload of teachers. The example here empowers reflective practitioners as '*re*-searchers' who 'look again' at their teaching practice more systematically, sharing their self-discoveries for others to learn from.

To summarise, the vignettes have demonstrated how decisions of senior leaders in particular contexts result in variable research practices and outcomes. Whilst there are clearly benefits of different types of PR, it is also important to note the challenges raised by the practitioners here so that future pathways for PR are successful.

Questions for the Reader

1. What does PR mean for you? Engaging *with* research, or engaging *in* your own research?
2. How might reflective practice be transformed into *re*-search?

References

Brown, C., Zhang, D., Xu, N., & Corbett, S. (2018). Exploring the impact of social relationships on teachers' use of research: A regression analysis of 389 teachers in England. *International Journal of Educational Research*, 89, 36–46. https://doi.org/10.1016/j.ijer.2018.04.003

Carr, W., & Kemmis, S. (2002). *Becoming critical: Education, knowledge and action research*. RoutledgeFalmer. (Original work published 1986.)

Department for Education (DfE). (2011). *Teachers' standards*. https://www.gov.uk/government/publications/teachers-standards

Department for Education (DfE). (2016, March). *Educational excellence everywhere*. https://www.gov.uk/government/uploads/system/uploads/attachment_data/file/508447/Educational_Excellence_Everywhere.pdf

Department for Education. (2016, July). *Standard for teachers' professional development*. https://www.gov.uk/government/publications/standard-for-teachers-professional-development

Evetts, J. (2013). Professionalism: Value and ideology. *Current Sociology Review*, 61(5–6), 778–796. https://doi.org/10.1177/0011392113479316

Foreman-Peck, L., & Heilbronn, R. (2018). Does action research have a future? A reply to Higgins. *Journal of Philosophy of Education*, 52, 126–143. https://doi.org/10.1111/1467-9752.12272

Godfrey, D., & Brown, C. (2018). How effective is the research and development ecosystem for England's schools? *London Review of Education*, 16(1), 136–151. https://doi.org/10.18546/LRE.16.1.12

Goodyear, V. A., Parker, M., & Casey, A. (2019). Social media and teacher professional learning communities. *Physical Education and Sport Pedagogy*, 24(5), 421–433. https://doi.org/10.1080/17408989.2019.1617263

Goswami, D., & Stillman, P. (1987). *Reclaiming the classroom: Teacher research as an agency for change*. Heinemann.

Hordern, J. (2016). Regions and their relations: Sustaining authoritative professional knowledge. *Journal of Education and Work*, 29(4), 427–449. https://doi:10.1080/13639080.2014.958653

Marsden, R. (2020). *Understanding research engagement in England's evidence-informed teaching profession: A '3D' view*. [Doctoral thesis, Liverpool John Moores University]. LJMU Research Online Repository. http://researchonline.ljmu.ac.uk/id/eprint/13836/

Maxwell, B., Greany, T., Aspinwall, K., Handscomb, G., Seleznyov, S. & Simkins, T. (2015). *Approaches to Research & Development for 'great pedagogy' and 'great CPD' in teaching school alliances*. National College for Teaching and Leadership. https://assets.publishing.service.gov.uk/media/5a7f4da940f0b6230268eaea/Approaches_to_research_and_development_for_great_pedagogy_and_CPD_in_TSAs.pdf

Research Schools Network. (n.d.). *Our aims*. https://researchschool.org.uk/about/our-aims

Royal Society & British Academy. (2018). *Harnessing educational research*. https://royalsociety.org/-/media/policy/projects/rs-ba-educational-research/educational-research-report.pdf

Thomas, L. (2017). The masters in teaching and learning: Lessons to be learnt and key stakeholder perceptions. *Teacher Education Advancement Network Journal*, 9(1), 45–55.

Wall, K., & Hall, E. (2017). The teacher in teacher-practitioner research: Three principles in inquiry. In P. Boyd & A. Splitz (Eds.), *Teachers and teacher educators learning through inquiry: International perspective*. https://www.academia.edu/33923746/Teachers_and_Teacher_Educators_Learning_Through_Inquiry_International_Perspectives

Winch, C., Oancea, A., & Orchard, J. (2013). *The contribution of educational research to teachers' professional learning – Philosophical understandings*. https://www.bera.ac.uk/wp-content/uploads/2014/02/BERA-Paper-3-Philosophical-reflections.pdf?noredirect=1

CHAPTER 5

The Cyclical Nature of Being Both 'Practitioner' and 'Researcher' and the Influence on Professional Development Design

Rebekah Gear[a] and Tazreen Kassim-Lowe[b]
[a]Nottingham Trent University, UK
[b]University of Nottingham, UK

ABSTRACT

The chapter explores the themes of identity, power and positionality through reflexive interviewing, where researchers can reflect on participant interactions and communicate nuanced ethical dilemmas (Olmos-Vega et al., 2023). Subjectivity is embraced whilst sharing extracts from reflexive interviews to consider what it means to be individuals, who exist in a third space between practice and research (Ostinelli, 2016, p. 542). Reflexivity is framed as a tool which develops Professional Development (PD) design.

Keywords: Professional development (PD); close-to-practice research; practitioner-research; positionality; reflexivity

Introduction

As former primary classroom practitioners, who operate in higher education and still teach in some capacity, we are not quite teachers nor academics but rather occupy a third space in between (Ostinelli, 2016). Through reflexively facilitating close-to-practice research in PD design, we explore the intersection between these practitioner and researcher identities.

We outline a case study of PD design where we actively encourage participants to adopt practitioner-researcher identities. Practitioner research can synthesise theory and practice and develop local solutions (Bell et al., 2010; Stenhouse, 1981; William, 2013). However, it can be undervalued due to time pressure, lack of resources and greater priorities (Kassim-Lowe & Gear, 2023). In interview extract 1, the first of multiple reflexive interview extracts throughout the chapter, we discuss other invalidating barriers, including a narrow view of researcher identity.

Extract 1

Rebekah: *I think some of the dilemmas was a lack of understanding and sometimes a discomfort between research being something that has to be funded and on a large scale or done by somebody that has a qualification like a Ph.D. I don't think it was seen as something that was necessarily important and valued....*

Tazreen: *(...)It sounds like a perception thing(...) who is a researcher?*

Reflexivity and PD Design

We chose to support teachers in conducting their own close-to-practice research by first taking part in collaborative live lesson research (LLR). We are aware that PD design, which features close-to-practice research, must consider the broader context and be robust and cyclical (Wyse et al., 2018, pp. 1–2). Additionally, practitioner-researcher identities were developed through 'doing' research but also 'being', through reflection. We encouraged participants to engage in professional noticing (Mason, 2002) as a first step towards researching their own practice (see extract 2).

Extract 2

Rebekah: *And I think that's the thing with research. It's that building of momentum in your practice. So(...)*

> *I think(...)it starts with noticing(...)and that's what we're doing all the time. We're always observing children. We're reflecting on practice, and we are hopefully reacting to that...*

In the PD design, research was positioned as something within reach, starting with noticing (Parsons, 2021). We supported participants in navigating the identity of both researcher and practitioner by engaging with and being critical of research with the knowledge that answers are not always the ambition (Stenhouse, 1981; Wyse et al., 2018). Instead, we emphasised the act of inquiry itself. We modelled what good professional noticing (Mason, 2002) and supportive reflexivity (Olmos-Vega et al., 2023) look like, as discussed in extract 3.

Extract 3

> **Tazreen:** *I think we tried to be really, really explicit about just how we work together...and then obviously supporting collaboration across phases across schools, within classrooms. But then another level, I think, is that we encourage the participants to support collaboration between their pupils.*

We aimed to work *with* as opposed to *on* participants by creating a democratic space where we acted as collaborators, facilitating close-to-practice research, as opposed to 'experts' (Wyse et al., 2018, pp. 1–2). Therefore, it was important to give participants time to reflect regularly about the research and their noticing habits to develop their own practitioner-researcher identities.

Noticing as a reflexive act, to connect researcher and practitioner identities, featured on multiple levels in the PD design:

- As facilitators, we used reflexive interviewing to notice and make decisions about how to address any power imbalances with participants.
- We asked participants to notice how we collaborated and modelled a critical and inquiring researcher mindset.
- We asked participants to notice aspects of their own practice.

- Through LLR, we asked participants to notice what learners noticed and how to facilitate better noticing to support learners in thinking mathematically.

Noticing Noticing

Noticing is a common thread between our reflexive PD design, participants' professional learning and learners' mathematical thinking. In extract 4, we discuss how noticing strengthened the link not only between research and practice, but with each other's ways of thinking.

> **Extract 4**
>
> **Tazreen:** *So how do you think we used noticing to support teachers and their own action research with our professional development?*
>
> **Rebekah:** *So we invited people to share what they noticed about the lesson and how it unfolded and the impact on the children and what I noticed was how when they were sharing what they observed and noticed they made connections with each other.*

The rich professional conversation generated from the LLR meant that participants' practitioner-research identities had the opportunity to synthesise; to develop beyond isolated consumers of research to collaborative appliers, analysers, and eventually innovators of their own practice (Mason, 2002).

Case Study: How Do I Promote Noticing?

The PD was designed around the theme of equity in mathematics targeting vulnerable pupils and facilitating more opportunities to think mathematically. The participants collaboratively planned a live research lesson to support pupil noticing inspired by Barclay (2021), who positioned low-attaining learners as valuable contributors. The lesson was based around the activity '*Spaceship*' from the book *Mathematical Challenges for Able Pupils* (Department for Education, 2000); purposefully chosen to reject deficit narratives. One participant acted as the model teacher whilst the others observed focus children. Afterwards we discussed the successes and barriers of promoting noticing.

Evaluation of LLR

The organisation of the LLR positioned the participants as active contributors; emphasising mutuality between ourselves and them. The model valued and validated all stakeholders and their noticing within the process, including the children themselves, one participant stating *'You can't not be good at noticing'*. A LLR model encouraged interaction with a real life classroom context through a process of research, application and reflection (Wyse et al., 2018, pp. 1–2). It enabled participants to think of us as collaborators, who support them in the facilitation of their own close-to-practice research, as opposed to 'experts' delivering PD (Wyse et al., 2018, pp. 1–2). Most successfully, the regular reflection meant that participants got 'try on' their practitioner-researcher identities before conducting close-to-practice research in their own classroom; seeing themselves as valid contributors, not merely consumers of research as discussed in extract 5.

Extract 5

Tazreen: *Yeah, but it's also the bi-bi-directionality, isn't it? Doesn't just have to be from the top coming down to trickling down to the classroom.*

However, through our reflexive interviewing, a number of power issues were highlighted. Firstly, as individuals affiliated with higher education settings, we had access to research articles that participants would not have otherwise had access to. On occasion, due to a lack of time, we chose to summarise research for participants with the option to access entire articles. Ultimately, we acted as 'gatekeepers' to research, which highlights the wider systemic accessibility issues around research for classroom based practitioner-researchers not affiliated with a higher education institution (Rycroft-Smith, 2022). We would encourage fellow PD designers to empower their participants to engage in research through promoting critical literacy in the first instance, and not take for granted the privilege of access to research. In response to these dilemmas, we made design decisions with care, collaboration and democracy at the centre; learning and researching *with* practitioner-researchers rather than *on* practitioner-researchers (Parsons et al., 2020).

Conclusion

The Current Landscape

There is a growing body of research that advocates the positive impact of being research-informed and supporting school improvement, including pupil outcomes (Groß Ophoff et al., 2023). In extract 6, we discuss connecting research to practice by facilitating and being advocates for close-to-practice research:

> **Extract 6**
>
> **Rebekah:** *As we early careers researchers to support collaboration with teachers in schools, so like we've just been reflecting upon, we've set up. I mean, if we think about the work group, for example, the work group was set up to connect research with practice. And so like we've just been reflecting on, I wonder whether we came under that idea of close-to-practice research.*

However, in the context of close-to-practice research, there seems to be an endorsed narrative that researchers and practitioners have conflicting identities (Hordern, 2020). Gripton and Williams (2023) consider this challenge further, deciphering the difference between different roles and responsibilities within PD. The default identity of PD leads in Mathematics Education is often a 'broker' who shares a cascade of knowledge rather than enabling purposeful collaboration which enables discovery and curiosity. This further endorses the narrative that one 'expert' has the answer. Collaborative PD creates a space for an inclusive and location-specific research agenda (Kelchtermans, 2021). From our experience, a shared research agenda formed PD that focussed on supporting the process of generating questions and tools to support inquiry, rather than encouraging participants to obtain answers from facilitators.

Ethics

Reflexive interviewing allowed us to make nuanced ethical decisions and create mutuality between ourselves and our participants (Olmos-Vega et al., 2023). We did not consider ourselves to be experts but rather collaborators, inviting thoughts and opinions, and facilitating the connection between practice and research by providing access (see extract 7) (Boylan, 2016).

> **Extract 7**
>
> **Tazreen:** *I think you've mentioned ethics before, but I think you were hesitantto use the word experts and I and I would be as well. (…) We never said 'We are the experts, listen to us!' It was never that kind of power dynamic. We tried to make sure it was a working with rather than working on relationship. I think that's what we were trying to get them to think about with the children as well.*

However, we were aware that this might not be the view of the participants who may hope for answers. We adopted a model of care ethics based on the idea of mutual respect and the *'recognition and appreciation of response'* (Noddings, 2012, p. 52). This idea not only informed our PD design and interaction with participants but also reflexive ethical reasoning where participants and ourselves considered how we speak about and to our learners as a reflection of our own care ethics and values (Boylan, 2016, p. 396).

Acknowledgements

Thank you to the National Centre for the Excellence in the Teaching of Mathematics (NCETM) for commissioning the project and to our colleagues who took part in the project.

References

Barclay, N. (2021). Valid and valuable: Lower attaining pupils' contributions to mixed attainment mathematics in primary schools. *Research in Mathematics Education, 23*(2), 208–225.

Bell, M., Cordingley, P., Isham, C., & Davis, R. (2010). *Report of professional practitioner use of research review: Practitioner engagement in and/or with research*. Retrieved January 30, 2023, from www.curee.co.uk/files/publication/1297423037/Practitioner%20Use%20of%20Research%20Review.pdf

Boylan, M. (2016). Ethical dimensions of mathematics education. *Educational Studies in Mathematics, 92*(3), 395–409.

Department for Education. (2000). *Mathematical challenges for able pupils: Bipods and tripods*. Crown.

Gripton, C., & Williams, H. (2023). The principles for appropriate pedagogy in early mathematics: Exploration, apprenticeship and sense-making. Part 1, Mathematics Teaching, issue 285 February 2023, 6–8.

Groß Ophoff, J., Brown, C., & Helm, C. (2023). Do pupils at research-informed schools actually perform better? Findings from a study at English schools. *Frontiers in Education, 7*, 1011241.

Hordern, J. (2020). Collaboration in educational research: Power, politics, and practice. *Educational Researcher, 49*(3), 183–192.

Kassim-Lowe, T. T., & Gear, R. (2023, Summer). From consumers to contributors. *BERA Research Intelligence, 15*, 14.

Kelchtermans, G. (2021). Keeping educational research close to practice. *British Educational Research Journal, 47*(6), 1504–1511.

Mason, J. (2002). *Researching your own practice, the discipline of noticing*. RoutledgeFalmer.

Noddings, N. (2012). The language of care ethics. *Knowledge Quest, 40*(5), 52.

Olmos-Vega, F. M., Stalmeijer, R. E., Varpio, L., & Kahlke, R. (2023). A practical guide to reflexivity in qualitative research: AMEE Guide No. 149. *Medical Teacher, 45*(3), 241–251.

Ostinelli, G. (2016). The many forms of research-informed practice: A framework for mapping diversity. *European Journal of Teacher Education, 39*(5), 534–549.

Parsons, S. (2021). The importance of collaboration for knowledge co-construction in 'close-to-practice' research. *British Educational Research Journal, 47*(6), 1490–1499.

Parsons, S., Yuill, N., Good, J., & Brosnan, M. (2020). 'Whose agenda? Who knows best? Whose voice?' Co-creating a technology research roadmap with autism stakeholders. *Disability & Society*, *35*(2), 201–234.

Rycroft-Smith, L. (2022). Knowledge brokering to bridge the research-practice gap in education: Where are we now? *Review of Education*, *10*, 1–46.

Stenhouse, L. (1981). What counts as research? *British Journal of Educational Studies*, *29*(2), 103–114.

William, D. (2013). Assessment: The bridge between teaching and learning. *Voices from the Middle*, (21), 15–20.

Wyse, D., Brown, C., Oliver, S., & Poblete, X. (2018). *The BERA close-to-practice research project: Research report*. British Educational Research Association.

CHAPTER 6

Three Lecturers, Three Universities, Three Countries: Can Facilitating Connecting Art Workshops in International Educational Contexts Create Connection and Criticality?

Frances-Ann Norton
Leeds Arts University, UK

ABSTRACT

This chapter explores the impact of an innovative arts-based workshop called *Connected Art* in universities in Germany, Spain and the UK and in three universities. The focus of the research method is a collaborative *close-to-practice* chapter involving 59 arts students. Readers will take away a practical teaching method designed to develop students' critical thinking within a practical paradigm. This chapter contributes to knowledge in co-developed pedagogic teaching strategies and practitioner research in arts education.

Keywords: Connected art; close-to-practice; critical thinking; community of inquiry; dérive; art pedagogy

Introduction

Meeting at an arts pedagogy conference, three arts-based lecturers from three countries embarked on a *close-to-practice* research project. Brown and Ergül (2024), in a conference on *close-to-practice* research, comment that *close-to-practice* develops the relationship between educational research and educational practice. *Close-to-practice* teaching and learning enables active involvement of researchers within their own practices, blending research, teaching and activism. There is a critique of *close-to-practice* as a methodology. Hordern (2021) and Deng (2024) write that *close-to-practice* can overlook accountabilities and elevate certain forms of knowledge production that might ignore core educational concerns. However, in this chapter, the positive benefits and impacts of *close-to-practice* are highlighted as useful in international educational contexts.

Discussion

Connected Art is a pedagogic method (Norton et al., 2024), offering participants one way to develop critical thinking. It facilitates participants to understand and apply complex theories to creative collaborative projects, through dialogue in a Community of Inquiry. This chapter adopts a qualitative, *close-to-practice*, constructivist (Vygotsky, 2012) paradigm in which a theoretical education method is put into practice. In constructivism, knowledge is built in an active process (Dewey, 2018). A hermeneutic epistemology (Gadamer, 2013), interprets findings utilising life-writing reflections (Wyse et al., 2021). Comment that *close-to-practice* research creates a praxis of educational theory and teaching practice. This is supported by academics across a number of disciplines (Barrett & Bolt, 2014; Broadhead & Gregson, 2018). In this chapter, my co-researchers in Germany and Spain and myself begin to fuse horizons, building joint understandings on the pedagogic implications of *Connected Art* method.

Three Lecturers, Three Universities, Three Countries

Connected Art Group One was enabled by a lecturer at a university in Germany it had 25 undergraduate participants from sustainability, environmental, political, economic sciences and pedagogy. Group Two was directed by a lecturer at a university in Spain with 21st-year fine art undergraduate participants. I facilitated Group Three at an arts school in the UK with 14 participants from advertising, fine art and textile design. In total, approximately 59 volunteer participants, with 3 lecturers, in 3 universities, across the 3 European countries.

What Is *Connected Art* Pedagogic Method?

Connected Art workshop asks participants to bring/make on the day/use found objects in the *taskscape* (Ingold, 2017) of the classroom, the countryside or urban metropolis, which analogises their arts practice or research interests. The workshop aims to be a cross-cutting and multifaceted pedagogic workshop facilitated by educator-practitioners. This is a research-engaged practice where there is an active seeking for answers to the research question through Aristotelian *Phronesis*. Broadhead and Gregson (2018) write compellingly about the educational good, the inclusive classroom that develops through operationalising *Phronesis*, practical wisdom. Putting to one side Cartesian dichotomies, Zundel and Kokkalis (2010) encourage educators to shift focus from separations of distinct realms of theory and practice towards an appreciation of the myriad of overlaps between academic and organisational practices. Physical objects are vibrant matter. Bennett (2020) theorises that a vital materiality courses through and across bodies, both human and non-human. Participants' objects are a vibrant form of understanding and research.

Randomly placing the objects, participants receive sticky notes and a ball of string. Like Theseus (of Greek mythology) in the labyrinth, they connect their object to other objects and participants with differently coloured string, finding a physical path and creating a web of interconnection as the strings criss-cross and intersect, creating a web of new understanding. Participants meet in a Community of Inquiry, which Garrison et al. (2000) state is a group of individuals who collaboratively engage in purposeful critical discourse and reflection to construct personal meaning and confirm mutual understanding. Dewey (in Xin, 2012, p. 20) sees Community of Inquiry as a philosophy of practice in education. He invites students to experience the world, education, art and politics as a way to think for themselves. Connecting Art Practice engenders Community of Inquiry creating a liminal (Sennett, 1998) threshold spaces for shaping community, free thinking, dialogue, movement and agency in education.

Participants move their bodies through the educational taskscape, using a Situationist International (a French art movement active between 1957 and 1972) concept of Dérive (1956) developed by Debord in Dérive participants drift, slowly studying and mapping the terrain and its inhabitants. Debord calls this psychogeography leading to new comprehensions of self and identity within liminal spaces. They are agential in their own pedagogic experience (Bernstein, 2000). For the educators they hope to generate knowledge from their pedagogic experience as data for the research. Participants may use critical, creative and caring thinking (Lipman, 2003) as they engage with Dérive and write down words and phrases from dialogue with each other. This creates a semantic field from which participants might move into further research, inspiration, dialogue, collaboration or arts practice. As Burke (2001) testifies from her own experience, participatory research becomes a co-creation of understanding, building knowledge through practical and dialogic methods.

Three Sites, One Method, Findings/Reflections

In this *close-to-practice* research, Group One in Germany. Participants completed this workshop over three days. Iteratively building on the initial objects and words, they developed; they then developed sustainable urban initiatives such as GoodLife RealLAB which enables real-world project, emphasising practitioner and public collaboration (Singer-Brodowski et al., 2018). Participants then used Dérive to navigate the urban landscape, collecting interviews with the public, which developed into sustainability projects. Participants commented that they felt they had to work very hard but that they enjoyed the whole experience, particularly developing connections through the initial objects between their own interests and those of their colleagues, overcoming shyness, interviewing strangers or being rejected several times helped participants overcome the perceived bubble of sustainability on campus. They were more able to get in touch with real-live people and real-world problems which helped initiate critical thinking about their own research. They developed a feeling of enjoyment, collaboration and investment in the group rather the competitiveness.

Group Two in Spain. The workshop resulted in sculptures and installations representing conceptual ideas related to the human body. These included the soul, issues of body dysmorphia and the experience of a kiss. Participants finally placed the sculptures back into the street, exploring this liminal space, an industrial unkempt urban area, which was the source of the original discarded waste materials which made the sculptures. Ideas and discussions around the theme of the body and its environment developed further and resulted in a public exhibition on sustainability. The exhibition featured body sculptures made from waste materials and a performance involving a piñata in the shape of an endangered seal, filled with beach waste. This manifested the critical thinking and creative process encouraged by the *Connected Art*.

Group Three in the UK. In my group, there was an initial wariness and resistance, a feeling of challenge and anxious to this project. Participants felt out of their comfort zone, some were at first confrontational and disruptive. Nevertheless, curiosity about the process helped them have perseverance and resilience. Through the workshop, they moved from tentative and apprehensive to open and confident. Participants reported being able to think about things differently, not overthinking, letting the process direct the flow. Another participant mentions that it offered an opportunity to discuss ideas without examination or module pressure.

These statements reveal the success of the workshop in developing and deepening their understanding of critical and caring thinking in their arts practice. Through discussion, they developed a semantic field of arts related words and phrases, which captured the moment in language. They used these words in later arts projects experimentally to try out new ideas and talk through their research in new ways, hermeneutically joining their horizons to create a larger worldview. *Connected Art* instilled confidence in academic research, articulation and critical in thinking through making.

The participants in the *close-to-practice* research in all three groups, in three countries, met hurdles they had to overcome. These were overcoming specialist subject-specific language in interdisciplinary work, allowing liminal spaces to engender clear creative and caring thinking in new student groups. To address wariness and confrontational behaviours, navigating the shift from high school to university or undergraduate to postgraduate study. Here, participants had to engage with unfamiliar peers, try a new and experimental pedagogic method and work with surprising interpersonal issues in collaborative contexts. These challenges can trigger fear of failure and a lack of self-confidence, when facing these challenges, particularly in the fields of arts education, relational and socially engaged art practices can offer transformative pedagogic contexts to connect people and ideas.

Conclusion

In Conclusion, Dear Reader...Do go to conferences and read academic texts such as this book. Connect, learn, share, be together as lecturer-researchers and be inspired to write about your own pedagogic *close-to-practice* experience. From our first meeting of the three lecturers at a conference, we decided to further develop and discuss *Connected Art* teaching method. We worked almost two years, on late-night-post-teaching Zoom sessions, to be able to get to this point of gathering together and reflecting on our experiences, and it is such a blessing. Conferences for busy lecturers are the points where horizontal and vertical discourse on pedagogy meet (Bernstein in Bourne, 2003). Where we can connect intellectually and in professional interpersonal relationships. Where practice research interests can be joined by life-writing/storytelling skills from the chalk face. The arts classroom can be a space for research-informed practice, where students and lecturers explore and link teaching and research, theory and practice. A space of transformation and a move towards knowledge mobilisation. In this space, we can share understandings of complex pedagogic theory such as Debord's theory of psychogeography and Dérive, or Ingold's anthropological writings on the taskscape. Where we can consider Dewey's genius in lifting experience to an academic audience or Bennett's post-human understanding of the connectedness and vibrancy of all matter. Most importantly, it's a place where we can discuss how we apply these concepts to our curriculum, our lectures and our symposia in the classroom to share with our learners.

I have found that *Connected Art* method that can develop Community of Inquiry by emphasizing social interaction, creative practices and transformative pedagogic experiences. There are some limitations to the method such as the challenge of transferring or generalising the findings from 59 participants to other educational settings. Also, the qualitative research design does not have statistical findings or include interdisciplinary, cross-cultural comparisons.

Despite these shortcomings, the three groups in UK, Germany and Spain, benefitted from the three lecturers sharing *Connected Art* method to enable them to establish deeply creative and complex learning environments that promoted social and personal interaction. The method also overcame potential barriers arising from the participants' many different cultural and disciplinary backgrounds, allowing participants to create practical, generative and creative projects addressing social issues such as sustainability in the arts.

Response to the Editorial Perspective

This chapter might act as a pedagogic guide for those educators, educational managers and curriculum developers wanting to explore practitioner research, *close-to-practice*, research-informed practice, participatory research or Research-engaged practice. It encourages early researchers and pedagogic practitioner researchers to investigate their own teaching contexts. It illustrates that by using educator's own experience and classrooms' knowledge, it can lead to a deeper understanding and development of teaching and learning. In conclusion, the Connected *Art* method engenders connection and community not only with lecturers when they work together but also with the students and educators that participate in the workshop.

Question for the Reader

How might the **Connected Art** method transform your own approach to teaching and learning in the arts, particularly in fostering collaboration and critical thinking across diverse, interdisciplinary contexts?

Ethics Statement

Ethical guidelines from the British Educational Research Association (BERA, 2024) were followed in recognising the diversity of contexts in the three international groups. Participants were treated fairly, and with freedom from bias. All participants were volunteers who gave informed consent. Participants, universities and lecturers are anonymised in the text so as to cause no harm. Participants had the right to withdraw from the research at any time. In addition, this chapter has ethical approval from the Ethics Committee at Leeds Arts University.

References

Barrett, E., & Bolt, B. (Eds.) (2014). *Practice as research: Approaches to creative arts enquiry*. Bloomsbury Publishing.
Bennett, J. (2020). *Vibrant matter: A political ecology of things*. Duke University Press.
Bernstein, B. (2000). *Pedagogy, symbolic control, and identity: Theory, research, critique*. Rowman & Littlefield.
Bourne, J. (2003). Vertical discourse: The role of the teacher in the transmission and acquisition of decontextualised language. *European Educational Research Journal*, 2(4), 496–521.
British Educational Research Association. (2024). *Ethical guidelines for educational research* (5th ed.). Retrieved February 22, 2025, from https://www.bera.ac.uk/publication/ethical-guidelines-for-educational-research-fifth-edition-2024

Broadhead, S., & Gregson, M. (2018). *Practical wisdom and democratic education: Phronesis, art and non-traditional students*. Springer Publishing.

Brown, N., & Ergül, H. (2024). *Social Fiction as a close-to-practice research approach* (Close to Practice Conference). Nottingham Trent University.

Burke, P. J. (2001). *Access/ing education: A feminist post/structuralist ethnography of widening educational participation*. Institute of Education University of London. PhD Dissertation.

Debord, G. (1956). "Theory of the Dérive". *Les Lèvres Nues #9* (Paris, November 1956). Reprinted in Internationale Situationniste #2 (Paris, December 1958). Translated by Ken Knabb. https://libcom.org/article/theory-derive-guy-debord

Deng, Z. (2024). Practice, pedagogy and education as a discipline: Getting beyond close-to-practice research. *British Educational Research Journal, 50*(2), 772–793.

Dewey, J. (2018). *How we think* (2nd ed.). Independent Publishing Platform, UK.

Gadamer, H. G. (2013). *Truth and method* (2nd ed.); Translated by Joel Weinsheimer and Donald G. Marshall. Bloomsbury Academic.

Garrison, D. R., Anderson, T., & Archer, W. (2000). Critical inquiry in a text-based environment. Computer conferencing in higher education. *Internet and Higher Education, 2000*(2), 87–105.

Hordern, J. (2021). Why close to practice is not enough: Neglecting practice in educational research. *British Educational Research Journal, 47*(6), 1451–1465.

Ingold, T. (2017). Taking taskscape to task. *Forms of Dwelling, 20*, 16–27.

Lipman, M. (2003). *Thinking in education* (2nd ed.). Cambridge University Press.

Norton, D., Norton, F. A., & Veciana, S. (2024). Connected art practice: Transformative learning environments for transdisciplinary competences. *Societies, 14*(3), 33.

Sennett, R. (1998). *The spaces of democracy* (pp. 40–41). University of Michigan, College of Architecture+ Urban Planning.

Singer-Brodowski, M., Beecroft, R., & Parodi, O. (2018). Learning in real-world laboratories: A systematic impulse for discussion. *GAIA-Ecological Perspectives for Science and Society, 27*(1), 23–27.

Vygotsky, L. S. (2012). *Thought and language* [Hanfmann, R., Vakar, G., Kozulin, A., Translator]. MIT Press.

Wyse, D., Brown, C., Oliver, S., & Poblete, X. (2021). Education research and educational practice: The qualities of a close relationship. *British Educational Research Journal, 47*(6), 1466–1489.

Xin, C. (2012). A critique of the community of inquiry framework. *Journal of Distance Education, 26*(1), 20–32.

Zundel, M., & Kokkalis, P. (2010). Theorizing as engaged practice. *Organization Studies, 31*(9–10), 1209–1227.

CHAPTER 7

Researching on the Inside Looking in: Navigating Issues of Power in Conducting Practitioner Research Projects

Sarah Peters[a] and Joyce I-Hui Chen[b]
[a]*Hull College, UK*
[b]*College of West Anglia, UK*

ABSTRACT

This chapter presents two separate action research (AR) projects in Further Education (FE) in England. One focuses on English for Speakers of Other Languages (ESOL) with adult learners and the other on Joint Practice Development (JPD) with teachers. Similar dilemmas about practitioner research (PR) and power issues in the workplace-as-research-site are noticed. Opportunities and limitations in professional practice alongside the pursuit of ethical research are explored.

Keywords: Action research; ESOL; ethics; JDP; power; practitioner research

Introduction

This chapter focuses on two action research (AR) projects undertaken in Further Education (FE) colleges in England. One considered an integrated skills pedagogy for adult ESOL (English for Speakers of Other Languages) using collaborative learning circles. The other explored the implementation of Joint Practice

Development (JPD) with FE teachers in professional learning. Both raised overlapping questions about practitioner research (PR) and navigating issues of power inside the workplace-research space.

We share our experiences of AR inquiries (McNiff, 2017; Stenhouse, 1981, 1985) between ourselves, our different workplaces and our positions within them (Biesta & Burbules, 2003). We consider our work-research positions in a 'third space' (Ostinelli, 2016, p. 542) between academic and practical knowledge.

First, we review the context of each project and explore issues of power as insider-researchers in FE. We provide examples of how our own roles may be restricted or enabled by the local context, how our positions may limit or expand opportunities for participants and how we seek appropriate methods for ethical practice (Mercer, 2007; Sikes & Potts, 2008). We conclude with lessons learned from the two projects regarding our PR, aiming to encourage on-going discussion for the enhancement of ethical PR practice.

Discussion

Inside Investigations

The FE sector in England is valued as a diverse educational provider, offering a wide range of learning and training opportunities and provisions (Gregson et al., 2020). FE plays an essential role to provide education, training and career opportunities to young people and adults in local communities. The range and levels of courses provided at FE colleges demonstrate the diverse needs of teachers, as well as learners who often enrol without minimum levels or grades in English or mathematics.

We both work in general FE colleges in England, situated in remote and coastal locations. The two colleges share similar characteristics of changing industries, shared community values and a focus on advancing the local economy.

In ESOL, the Skills for Life (DfES, 2001) legacy symbolises education as a means to develop economically active citizens, minimising personal learning needs and other viewpoints. This raises questions about power relationships and sanctioned voices. Circles enable students to influence classroom content and interactions through small group discussions and feedback to responsive teachers.

For the JPD project, financial constraints such as budget cuts see many colleges forced to merge and reduce expenditure on resources and equipment, including recruiting and training high-quality staff (Keohane, 2017). Yet FE teachers have been 'persuaded' to embrace the changes, implement new initiatives and maintain quality teaching, learning, and assessment (TLA). This project aims to implement a different and democratic model of professional learning.

Tightening national parameters for 'good' quality teacher education and pedagogy, such as the Education Inspection Framework (Ofsted, 2024), cause us to reflect on the purpose of education and our roles within it. We value education as a general benefit for individuals and society at large, having deeper personal significance and culturally richer meaning than national economic goals, which asks questions of how we see ourselves in our roles, working with others and for others. Adopting a sustained, self-critical and systematic (Stenhouse, 1981, 1985) AR approach, we reflect on our contexts, plan for and implement a change in response to local conditions, review and adapt our actions (McNiff, 2017). Addressing issues of power as insider-researchers in FE and upholding our democratic beliefs are integral to this process.

A shared power consideration was obtaining approval to commence AR. This required us to write business cases for our HR departments and senior managers linked to quality improvement plans. Initially, the ESOL project was rejected centrally but approved at a departmental level. Success was due to existing pragmatic understanding (Biesta & Burbules, 2003) of how AR could potentially benefit ESOL pedagogy, CPD and strategic concerns. Therefore, our immediate managers were supportive of PR but within the limits of our existing roles, leading to a second issue of negotiating time and resources for research. Joining the ETF/SUNCETT PhD programme, gave us external support and validation to carve out space inside our settings.

Being inside, we have direct access to the workplace, contact with people, and understanding of our contexts and cultures, saving time and budget looking for suitable settings and participants (Sikes & Potts, 2008). We hold pre-existing trusting relationships, meaning we are familiar with 'the language' used by participants and can 'empathise' with the scenarios they are in. Therefore, participants are willing to share their true stories (Atkins & Wallace, 2012).

Investigating workplace issues with our own students and colleagues involves managing multiple identities and relationships as a staff member, a colleague, a friend, a teacher, a researcher and a participant. Greene (2014, p. 7) contends that an insider-researcher 'must be able to shift between identities and their dual roles of researcher and the researched, but without causing a noticeable disturbance to the research setting'.

Therefore, it is crucial to thoroughly consider our own positions in the process of planning and engagement with participants, and to take considerate steps to ensure credibility and reliability of data (Atkins & Wallace, 2012). It is important to consider what techniques and tools can help maintain the balance of viewing different perspectives and opinions with an 'unbiased' lens, as conducting PR inside a familiar environment means that 'preconceptions may colour accounts, because so much more is already known (or thought to be known)' (Mercer, 2007, p. 8).

For this, we recognise our power positions as the professional 'experts' in our respective projects. Both risk an overly controlled approach, with the PR being the sole-decision maker (Dunne, 1993), if we do not listen and respond to participant feedback. As a balance to our positions of relative power in the research process but limited in the wider hierarchy, our PR weaves collective but diverse participant voices and mixed-methods data into our investigations.

Quantitative evidence, such as assessment results, is comfortably recognised by managers who control time and resources. Qualitative data from field notes, participant reflective diaries, transcripts and semi-structured interviews permeate metrics. Mixed data looks for meaningful holistic results where 'The sense of the whole is built from a rich data source with a focus on the concrete particularities of life that create powerful narrative tellings' (Connelly & Clandinin, 1990, p. 5).

Narratives make a situation recognisable and reveal entrenched power dynamics and social relationships (Habermas, 1972). Our PR includes an emancipatory purpose for research, allowing people to question accepted norms and to take action. Key to this is a participatory approach to be inclusive and democratic in our recording of and responses to data.

Striving for ethical PR, we seek appropriate methods, data collection and reporting. It is essential that we seek to understand participants' perspectives and not to impose our own interpretations on individual experiences. Reflecting on how all participants contribute to maximise views and layering them with quantitative information is a way to look for key impacts above external prescriptions and to neutralise our own positions.

Additionally, our PR places us in a 'third space' (Ostinelli, 2016) where our own and participants' individual, local, practical understandings meet academic knowledge. A methodical and rigorous AR process connects our real-world practice to more widely accepted theory.

From our PR, we have learnt that researching as insiders undercuts local and wider hierarchies as we initiate and lead projects, gaining professional agency. However, as project managers, we may potentially impose research on others, raising the consideration of ethics of power.

There is power imbalance in the teacher/researcher-student/researched relationship. This urges us to take care: to be caring towards participants sharing their work, experiences and reflections (Lipman, 2003); to handle data carefully and with consent (Ghaye, 2011). Each project document and interaction is a potential focus of reflection and judgement made possible and credible from the 'historical consciousness' (Carr, 2006, p. 430) of our insider positions and aiming to maximise participant voice.

Conclusion and Reflection on the Editorial Perspective

Reflecting on the editorial perspective, this chapter considers PR within FE as centring on ethical considerations, power dynamics and the interplay of academic and practical knowledge.

We advocate for reflective AR grounded in an ethic of care to empower educators and learners.

Current direction in FE in England elevates an education-for-employment view which we navigate in search of meaningful educational experiences and outcomes for learners. It is by reflecting on our work roles that we consider alternative practice. This is an act of resistance made possible by a reflective AR process inside our settings.

Developing teachers' ability in their practice and improving students' language skills supports current and potential employees to work and contribute economically to society. However, this misses a wider and deeper potential that enriches and empowers individuals in a critical, enquiring society to communicate and learn together.

In order to implement our projects, it is necessary to negotiate and persuade the gatekeepers and allies of our roles. For this we need hard evidence, such as quality improvement plans or achievement data that support the need for and demonstrate success for the projects. However, such data may only play a supporting role to the core values that spur PR.

The purpose of the projects needs to be communicated with clarity to be understood by a diverse audience: managers, colleagues, funders, a wider research community and participants. Yet, PR needs to remain flexible as outcomes may vary considerably to those initially anticipated. A reflective PR process involves continually thinking and re-thinking about actions and reactions with other active participants.

The success of these projects also rests on relationships. An insider-researcher needs to foster meaningful relationships with participants. This aspect of conducting PR develops a trusting and trustworthy connection between participants and ourselves as colleagues-teachers-researchers, not just close-to-practice but deep within it.

The themes and findings derived from the projects support the notion of an ethic of care as the underpinning principle of all activities. The Ethical Guidelines of BERA (2024) specify that no harm should be imposed upon the participants, for example ensuring informed consent to participate and how collected data is handled. This has an important implication to participatory AR projects such as these studies.

Critical reflection and developing conclusions are never complete. Constantly re-visiting and re-evaluating with the people around us may offer a better understanding of teacher development, language classroom interactions, and professional roles. We understand that our work-research positions bridge academic and practical knowledge, in which we consciously reflect on our ethics and values to better understand ourselves and our multiple, intersecting roles, and to contribute to directions for future practice to make a difference for learners and wider society.

Question for the Reader

What openings and/or barriers exist in your practice and setting for ethical research?

References

Atkins, L., & Wallace, S. (2012). *Qualitative research in education*. SAGE.

Biesta, G., & Burbules, N. C. (2003). *Pragmatism and educational research*. Rowman & Littlefield.

British Educational Research Association. (2024). *Ethical guidelines for educational research* (5th ed.). https://www.bera.ac.uk/publication/ethical-guidelines-for-educational-research-fifth-edition-2024

Carr, W. (2006). Philosophy, methodology and action research. *Journal of Philosophy of Education*, 40(4), 421–435.

Connelly, F. M., & Clandinin D. J. (1990). Stories of Experience and Narrative Inquire. *Educational Researcher*, 19(5), 2–14.

Department of Education and Skills (DfES). (2001). *Skills for Life – the national strategy for improving adult literacy and numeracy skills Delivering the vision 2001-2004*. https://dera.ioe.ac.uk/7187/7/ACF35CE_Redacted.pdf

Dunne, J. (1993). *Back to the rough ground. Practical judgement and the Lure of Technique*. University of Notre Dame Press.

Ghaye, T. (2011). *Teaching and learning through reflective practice: A practical guide for positive action*. Routledge.

Greene, M. J. (2014). On the inside looking in: Methodological insights and challenges in conducting qualitative insider research. *The Qualitative Report*, *19*(29), 1–13.

Gregson, M., Duncan, S., Brosnan, K., Derrick, J., Husband, G., Nixon, L., Spedding, P., Stubley, R., & Webber Jones, R. (2020). *Reflective teaching in further, adult and vocational education* (5th ed.). Bloomsbury.

Habermas, J. (1972). *Knowledge and human interests*. Heinemann.

Keohane, N. (2017). *Rising to the challenges: The further education and skills sector over the next decade*. The Social Market Foundation.

Lipman, M. (2003). *Thinking in education*. Cambridge University Press.

McNiff, J. (2017). *Action research: All you need to know*. Sage.

Mercer, J. (2007). The challenges of insider research in educational institutions: Wielding a double-edged sword and resolving delicate dilemmas. *Oxford Review of Education*, *33*(1), 1–17.

Ofsted. (2024). *Education inspection framework*. https://www.gov.uk/government/publications/education-inspection-framework

Ostinelli, G. (2016). The many forms of research-informed practice: A framework for mapping diversity. *European Journal of Teacher Education*, *39*(5), 534–549. http://dx.doi.org/10.1080/02619768.2016.1252913

Sikes, P., & Potts, A. (2008). *Researching education from the inside*. Routledge.

Stenhouse, L. (1981). What counts as research? *British Journal of Educational Studies*, *29*(2), 103–114. https://doi.org/10.1080/00071005.1981.9973589

Stenhouse, L. (1985). *Research as a basis for teaching: Readings from the work of Lawrence Stenhouse*. Heinemann.

CHAPTER 8

Teachers Teaching Teachers

Sylvia Ikomi
University of Leeds, UK

ABSTRACT

This chapter explores the positive impact that the intersections of practitioner researchers' identities can have on teachers' engagement with their work. It considers the impact of being an insider through having a shared racial, cultural and professional experience with the teachers that research is being shared with. It explores the impact of being an insider on the level of authority that a practitioner-researcher is afforded by teachers and on the ways in which the teachers' respond to practitioner-researchers' research. The chapter explores these issues through a reflection on positive observations that a Black, female, teacher made from her Continuous Professional Development (CPD) sessions with teachers on the adultification of Black girls.

Keywords: Practitioner-researcher; intersections; identity; Black girls; adultification; adultification-bias

Introduction

This chapter explores how research practitioners' identity, power and positionality when engaging with teachers is affected by the intersectionality of practitioner-researchers' identities. Can identity lead to a sense of belonging when speaking to a group of teachers and how does this lead to a deeper engagement from teachers? Does it have the potential to enrich the level of knowledge exchange between a practitioner-researcher and the teachers they share their research with? My reflection on my experience of delivering 'CPD' sessions to teachers on the adultification of Black girls addresses these questions.

My Identity and My Work

Alison Griffith defines an insider as 'someone whose biography (gender, race, class, sexual orientation and so on) gives her a lived familiarity with the group being researched' (Griffith, 1998, p. 361). My professional identity is multifaceted. I am a secondary school teacher, Higher Education lecturer and PhD student. I am a Black woman whose research specialism is on a key topic that affects Black girls and affected me when I was growing up: the adultification of Black girls. My PhD research is on the adultification of Black girls and includes an exploration of how the education system can address the issue of the adultification-bias that some teachers have towards Black girls that has a detrimental impact on Black girls (including Black girls in state care). In 2022, I developed a case study (Ikomi, 2023) on the adultification of Black girls within the education system that was anchored on the case of Child Q (a Black girl that was infamously strip searched by police officers in a school in London, CHSCP, 2022). I started delivering CPD Sessions on this issue for teachers in 2022.

Discussion

Teaching Black Teachers

I have delivered my CPD session on the adultification of Black girls within the education system to teachers that were attending a conference for Black teachers. While the wider academic conversation on the adultification of Black girls, often centres on the adultification-bias that they experience at the hand of white professionals, Black girls also experience adultification-bias from Black people. My case study on the adultification of Black girls within the education system and my Churchill Fellowship study (Ikomi, 2024) on the adultification of Black girls in state care incorporate Linda Burton's conceptual model of adultification within the dynamic between a parent and a child

(Burton, 2007). Burton's conceptual model identifies key elements of a dynamic in which a child takes on the role of the responsible adult in their relationship with their parent and the parent takes on the role of the child as manifested through: parentification (a process in which the child takes on the role of the parent), spousification (the child takes on the role of a spouse) and peerification (the child takes on the role of a peer of the same age rather than a child) (Burton, 2007). I discovered an additional advantage of addressing this issue with Black teachers during my CPD session. The Black teachers at the conference that I attended had multifaceted roles that connected them to my topic: as teachers who taught Black girls, teachers who observed their colleagues who were not Black teaching Black girls through their lens as professionals who share similar characteristics and cultural similarities with the girls, as parents, aunties, uncles, cousins, sisters and grandparents of Black girls. I mentioned my lived experience of adultification within my own family (following a family crisis) with the teachers. This provided the teachers with an opportunity to see that my expertise in the topic not only derived from my academic research but from my own lived experience, which, coupled with my status as a teacher, positioned me as someone from the inside discussing this issue.

The teachers were comfortable enough to raise issues of challenges they were having connected to their position as Black teachers that hampered their ability to effectively advocate for Black children that were experiencing adultification-bias from teachers. They expressed the challenge of being ignored, labelled as having an exaggerated over-identification with the children and how this in some instances culminated in hostility from their colleagues towards them (victimisation – when someone is punished for raising a complaint). The teachers opened up about the dynamic of home situations that contribute to Black girls' adultification within their parental dynamic with their parents before going into local authority care and the need for parents dealing with the challenges of being single parents to have more support. The teachers' expressed remorse for times they themselves unwittingly adultified Black girls within schools and have contributed to the problem. The teachers embraced the CPD session and were keen for the CPD session to lead to practical change for Black girls. I believe that being an 'insider' as a Black woman who has experienced adultification myself and a Black teacher supported me in receiving a rich level of engagement from my attendees.

Teaching Teachers

I have received a rich level of engagement from non-Black teachers when sharing my work. I have benefited from my vantage point of not just being a teacher but being a teacher who is closely affiliated with the key challenges in the area of recruitment and retention that secondary schools in England are facing due to the supply/substitute teaching that I have been doing since 2018. I am keenly aware of the anxiety that teachers often feel when it comes to working with children that have had an adverse childhood experience. This coupled with my knowledge of the pressure that schools that are in crisis-mode following a damning OFSTED report and longstanding recruitment and retention challenges are under and how this can manifest in a toxic working culture, means that I have been fortunate enough to not face some of the defensive responses that some academics experience when presenting research of this nature to an overworked and stressed group of teachers.

My engagement with teachers has broadened my understanding of how the issues that I am exploring in my PhD study affect them and potential barriers to their effective application of research of this nature to their work. It is my hope that my identity as a practitioner-researcher is something that I will draw on at all stages of my PhD to address some of the potential barriers that emerge when academics teach teachers.

Conclusion

There is an ongoing debate within academia about the pros and cons of insider-led research (Crean, 2018; Dwyer & Buckle, 2009; Mercer, 2007; Phillippo & Nolan, 2024). While being an insider when conducting and sharing research can create some limitations, the positive impact that it can have in supporting researchers to enhance CPD sessions with teachers as an opportunity to have a two-way exchange of rich knowledge, should not be under-estimated. In a social climate in which teachers are often heavily criticised and many are dealing with the demands of the longstanding issues of low teacher retention levels and high turnover rates and shifting education policy based on academics' latest research; teachers can be wary of researchers raising challenging issues without having the challenging professional and personal lived experience that they have had. Receiving research findings from a relatable researcher can support the building of bridges instead of walls between academia and teachers at a time when this bridge is urgently needed.

Response to the Editorial Perspective

A hallmark of practitioner research is that it leads to the development of research that is applied in practical ways. The context in which the work is used is often complex and is underpinned by contextual issues that cannot be adequately grasped without an in-depth engagement with the relevant institutions and their working culture. Practitioner research calls for research that does this, for example, through an effective harnessing of the researcher's positionality as an insider. A central tenet of effective practitioner research is a recognition that the researcher is not simply the fountain of all knowledge that is bestowing their academic knowledge on the professionals that are affected by their work; but is also a student that is developing their own understanding of the reality of the problems that they are addressing through the perspective of the professionals that are involved in the work. The importance of this has been underscored to me by my interaction with teachers during my CPD sessions. A stumbling block to the two-way knowledge exchange between researchers and the stakeholders that are affected by researchers' work can be the tension between academia's received wisdom on a topic and the views of stakeholders. Practitioner researcher's dual role supports us in recognising the value of the perspective of stakeholders that are on the ground, even when their views challenge academia's received wisdom on a topic. For example, on the surface there is an argument that the issue of teachers' adultification-bias towards Black girls can be addressed through the increased employment of Black teachers. However, Black teachers have shared the challenges that they can experience in advocating for these girls with me, reflecting the limitations of this approach. Continuous reflective practice that challenges overly simplistic assumptions and employs rich critical intellectualism is essential for effective practitioner research.

References

Burton, L. (2007). Childhood adultification in economically disadvantaged families: A conceptual model. *Family Relations*, 56(4), 329–345. https://onlinelibrary.wiley.com/doi/full/10.1111/j.1741-3729.2007.00463.x

City of London and Hackney. (2022). *Local child safeguarding practice review: Child Q*. [online]. https://chscp.org.uk/wp-content/uploads/2022/03/Child-Q-PUBLISHED-14-March-22.pdf

Collins, P. (2022). *Black feminist thought: Knowledge, consciousness, and the politics of empowerment* (2nd ed). Routledge.

Crean, M. (2018). Minority scholars and insider-outsider researcher status: Challenges along a personal, professional and political continuum. In *Forum qualitative sozialforschung/forum: Qualitative social research* (Vol. 19, No. 1, p. 16). DEU. https://www.ssoar.info/ssoar/handle/document/71913

Dwyer, S. C., & Buckle, J. L. (2009). The space between: On being an insider-outsider in qualitative research. *International Journal of Qualitative Methods*, 8(1), 54–63. https://journals.sagepub.com/doi/full/10.1177/160940690900800105

Griffith, A. I. (1998). Insider/outsider: Epistemological privilege and mothering work. *Human Studies*, 21(4), 361–376.

Ikomi, S. (2023). Child Q: A case study of the adultification of Black Girls in schools. *The European Conference on Education*, 17–25. https://papers.iafor.org/proceedings/conference-proceedings-ECE2023/

Ikomi, S. (2024). *The Adultification of Black girls in state care: Perspectives*. Churchill Fellowship. https://www.churchillfellowship.org/ideas-experts/ideas-library/the-adultification-of-black-girls-in-state-care-perspectives/

Mercer, J. (2007). The challenges of insider research in educational institutions: Wielding a double-edged sword and resolving delicate dilemmas. *Oxford Review of Education*, *33*(1), 1–17. https://www.tandfonline.com/doi/full/10.1080/03054980601094651

Phillippo, K. L., & Nolan, J. L. (2024). White-on-white research: A study of white qualitative researcher positionality among white participants. *International Journal of Qualitative Studies in Education*, *37*(2), 545–563. https://www/tandfonline.com/doi/full/10.1080/09518398.2022.2061728

Introduction to Section 3: Professional Learning and Sharing Skills

Joyce I-Hui Chen
College of West Anglia, UK

This section examines diverse approaches to professional learning, research-informed practice, and the development of educator identities. It explores how practitioners integrate theory and practice through collaboration, reflective inquiry, and evidence-based approaches, addressing challenges in educational contexts.

In the chapter 'Developing Professional Knowledge as a Consortium: Moving from "I" to "We"' by RATED Consortium, Claire Haresnape Tyson, Matthew J. Easterbrook, Lewis Doyle, Alison Glover, Elizabeth Hidson, and Thomas Perry, the RATED Consortium uses evidence-based strategies to tackle educational inequalities, operating in the 'third space' between research and practice. A key initiative involves addressing unconscious teacher bias through a co-created rubric and video-based critical reflection. The consortium emphasises shared values, mutual respect, and an ecosystem model for collaborative problem-solving, exemplifying successful practitioner-research partnerships.

In the chapter 'An Insider Perspective: Exploring Teachers' Engagement with Professional Development in Cooperation with Practitioner Co-Researchers', Marianne Talbot identifies barriers to teacher professional development (PD), such as financial constraints, lack of supply cover, and unsupportive leadership. Effective PD must be accessible, relevant, and autonomy-supporting. Through qualitative surveys and roundtable discussions, Talbot highlights strategies to overcome these challenges, focusing on trust, agency, and reflective collaboration to enhance engagement.

The chapter 'The Research-Engaged Practitioner: The Importance of Research Literacy and Critical Reflection for the Novice Teacher's Professional Learning' by Leanne Henderson, Danyah Alsayeud, and Ian Collen focuses on the role of Initial Teacher Education (ITE) in fostering research literacy and reflective practices among novice teachers. Using frameworks like Dewey's reflective practice and action research, the authors describe interventions that help trainees bridge theoretical and practical divides. They argue for integrating critical self-reflection and evidence-informed practices to empower teachers as lifelong learners.

In the chapter 'The Journey Towards a Whole-School Culture of Teachers as Researchers: Reflections from a State-Maintained School for Students with Special Educational Needs and Disabilities' by Hannah Lovatt and Gina Stafford, Rumworth School's case study details the evolution of a teacher-research model in a SEND (Special Educational Needs and Disabilities) context. Transitioning from autonomous inquiry to structured research cycles, the school addressed key areas like feedback and observation practices. This collaborative approach highlights the benefits of balancing autonomy with guided inquiry to foster professional growth and inclusivity.

In the chapter 'Developing Research-Informed Trainee Teachers', Dr Elizabeth Hidson advocates for situational verification in teacher training to connect research with practice. Trainees engage in school-based interventions and action research, refining pedagogical strategies like behaviour management through evidence-based inquiry. By cultivating research literacy and a questioning mindset, this approach develops trainee teachers as practitioner-researchers capable of contributing to system-wide improvements.

The chapter 'Disrupting to Develop' by Debbie Bogard, Freya Cox-Willmott, and Neil Hart highlights a Sixth Form College's community of practice model, which disrupts traditional hierarchies through distributed leadership and peer-led initiatives. Projects like 'Talking to Learn' demonstrate the power of co-created research and align with bell hooks' vision of education as a practice of freedom. The approach reshapes professional identities, fostering inclusive, participatory learning.

Together, these chapters illustrate the transformative potential of professional learning communities, research-practice partnerships, and reflective practices. They offer a roadmap for building inclusive, equitable, and research-informed educational environments that empower teachers and learners alike.

CHAPTER 9

The Journey Towards a Whole-School Culture of Teachers as Researchers: Reflections from a State-Maintained School for Students with Special Educational Needs and Disabilities

Hannah Lovatt[a] and Gina Stafford[b]
[a]University of Greater Manchester, UK
[b]Rumworth School, Bolton, UK

ABSTRACT

This chapter presents a critical reflection on the process of setting up a whole-school model for teacher research. It is a collaborative piece presented through the lens of the school's senior lead for CPD, co-written with a university lecturer. The chapter details the implementation of, and learnings from, yearly, school-wide, practitioner-research cycles that occurred prior to the inception of the Research-Practice Partnership (RPP) with the University of Greater Manchester. The chapter concludes that such a partnership might enrich the school's teacher-research cycles.

Keywords: Special Educational Needs and Disability (SEND); research-practice partnership; teacher-research model; yearly reflections; broad themes; implementation

Introduction

This chapter presents a case study of Rumworth School, a state-maintained SEND secondary school in Northwest England. It describes the school's process of initiating a whole-school teacher-research model for professional development, in which the teachers are guided to conduct their own practice-based enquiry. Schools are increasingly expected to develop research-informed and evidence-informed practice (DfE, 2016; Ovenden-Hope, 2024; Stoll, 2015). The implementation of action-research models has been shown to enhance educators' professional autonomy, develop resilience, and facilitate engagement in knowledge exchange with wider educational communities (de Paor & Murphy, 2018; Kennedy, 2005; Wilson, 2012).

Rumworth's enrolment count has more than doubled since 2015. The demographic now encompasses a wider range of learners with complex needs, with significant implications for school organisation and management, the design of curricula, and approaches to professional learning.

Reflecting on the 50 years since the introduction of Stenhouse's 'teacher as researcher' concept (Stenhouse, 1975, p. 142), we describe how this form of professional learning can address contemporary issues facing schools and the impact of the fast expansion of the special school sector (DfE, 2024b; National Audit Office, 2019).

Initiation of the Whole-School Strategy to Enhance Practice-Based Enquiry

The challenges of Rumworth's changing learner demographics and staff recruitment necessitate changes in the school's existing model for professional learning, and the implementation of a whole-school, group-based, teacher-research model. Learners with SEND have diverse and often, multiple needs and unique learning preferences (National Audit Office, 2019; Office for National Statistics, 2022) and as such, teachers at Rumworth have developed rich, fluid, and diverse contextual 'know-how'. The Senior Leadership Team (SLT) felt that the 'situated knowledge of practitioners' needed greater appreciation and the teachers' tacit 'know how' should be made more explicit (Guldberg et al., 2017, p. 396; Wilson, 2012).

The overarching aim was to establish self-sustaining, habitual, collegial and contextually responsive practices of classroom enquiry to highlight teacher 'wisdom' through communities-of-practice within the school's working environment. The aspirational aim is to expand this outward and develop local school partnerships which provide a platform for knowledge exchange and enhance provision for SEND pupils through tested, evaluated and shared best-practice.

The Total Autonomy Model

Teacher-Research Cycle 1 (2018)

In this introductory year, the primary consideration was to develop teacher trust, interest and 'buy-in' for our new way of engaging in professional learning. A total-autonomy, teacher-led model was adopted: teachers were able to dictate the aims and methods of enquiry which resulted in high levels of interest, engagement and widespread participation. However, at the end-of-cycle dissemination event findings were mostly anecdotal rather than systematic and rigorous; a finding not uncommon for action-research in schools (Kallitsoglou & Mahmud, 2023). Post-cycle evaluations encouraged SLT to reflect on the need to design a model to effectively develop the knowledge and skills needed to conduct high-quality, systematic and rigorous group enquiry while ensuring it was operationally feasible and contextually responsive.

A Structured Theory Model

Teacher-Research Cycle 2 (2019)

In response to the lack of rigour in the previous cycle, the school designated a specific educational theory to guide teacher-research. This cycle was titled 'An enquiry into the use of Rosenshine's 10 Principles of Educational Instruction' (Rosenshine, 2012). This pedagogical framework was chosen for its wide popularity in the school sector, where it is claimed to 'serve as a highly accessible bridge between research and practice' (Sherrington, 2019, p. 7). Collaborative teacher groups selected one principle of instruction and conducted peer observations to evaluate the extent to which practice might be improved.

The cycle fostered an increasingly systematic and rigorous approach, but feedback from teachers was varied. Some found the principles a welcome and supportive framework, while others struggled to apply it to their situated practice. Some stated that the principles were already present in their practice and therefore did not lead to any specific impact or present new questions. Leaders welcomed the successes of the cycle, but considered how the model may have limited teacher autonomy and minimised the contextual and situational factors unique to the SEND classroom that inform questions of practice.

Covid Recalibration

Teacher-Research Cycle 3 (2020)

Amid the COVID-19 outbreak, the cycle underwent a 'recalibration'. The leadership team focused on the urgent issues of children's safety, wellbeing, learning and heightened staff workloads. A full teacher-research cycle was considered 'out-of-reach'. Instead, the cycle platformed critical peer-feedback skills, which were moulded around the pressing need to implement 'distancing-friendly' processes and creating and reviewing school documentation associated with statutory, Education, Health and Care Plan (EHCP) annual review meetings. We proposed this as a necessary feature of any contextually responsive professional development model and effectively 'held the space' until circumstances improved.

Teaching-Observation Redesign: Deconstructing the 'Outstanding'

Teacher-Research Cycle 4 (2021)

Progressive learnings led to the introduction of a broad theme for enquiry aimed at standardising and improving guidance to make the model operationally feasible, responsive to development needs and workload friendly. The post-covid sentiment fuelled a 'review and reorientation of *outstanding* teaching and learning at Rumworth'. The aim was to draw on the contextual expertise of teachers to deconstruct and reconstruct notions of outstanding teaching, better reflecting shifts in practice, resulting from the school's changing demographics. Teachers used phased peer-observation and critical dialogue, alongside the Teaching Standards (DfE, 2011), to revise criteria housed in the school-wide teaching observation proforma utilised by leaders, in their review of teaching quality. This process transformed the criteria from finite and reductive phrases, to those that were broader, more fluid and learner-dependent. The cycle fostered greater ownership of practice and a collective responsibility for teaching quality; teacher interest and investment were palpable, resulting in the highest level of engagement of all the cycles.

Feedback: What Does Better Look Like?

Teacher-Research Cycle 5 (2022)

We assigned feedback as the broad theme for this cycle, as gaps had emerged in our understanding of school-wide feedback practices resulting from our changing staff and student cohort, in recognition of the importance of feedback for achievement and learning (Mandouit & Hattie, 2023). Teacher-enquiry into feedback practices precipitated a feedback 'redesign' which better reflected the needs of new and existing learners and encourage expertise sharing across the ever-growing teaching team. Through peer-observation, teachers appraised the feedback processes and used this to inform each other's practice in the classroom. This cycle introduced the Teaching and Learning conference, the first formal event for sharing research process, interventions and findings from the teacher-research.

Critical Reflections and Learnings

Broad Theme for Enquiry, Teacher Autonomy and Knowledge Dissemination

Post-cycle evaluations confirmed that assigning a broad theme to each cycle improved guidance and scaffolding, enhanced the validity and rigour of teacher-research and reduced demand and workload. Critical reflections revealed that the choice of theme played a pivotal role in the quality of teacher-inquiries, levels of motivation and engagement, and overall success of the cycle.

The broad themes, such as 'teaching-observation redesign' and 'feedback', appeared to provide teachers with more options to pursue professional interests in practice-based problems at Rumworth. Cycle reflections mirror findings from literature, which show teachers' enhanced engagement in their professional development, if the interventions are embedded in their professional and working contexts (Admiraal et al., 2019; de Paor & Murphy, 2018).

School leaders recognised that the nascent stage of the school's teacher-research model may have precipitated issues in the workability of Rosenshine's principles. The school's model had yet to provide teachers with the knowledge and skills needed to perform the substantial task of interpreting and applying research evidence, while engaging in a robust and rigorous process of practice-enquiry. Teachers were expected to 'lead the way' in being 'critical consumers of evidence', via their processes of research translation, their own unique pedagogies and other research evidence (Bokhove & Hyde, 2024, p. 37). Some creative tensions echo Müller and Cook's (2024) proposal that findings from cognitive science are not easily applied to classroom practice, owing to context-specificity and the ineliminable variables of learning conditions and student characteristics.

When adopting broad themes, we ensured they underwent an appraisal of 'workability'. When this notion of 'reconnaissance' is applied, the theme goes through a process of consideration, consultation and review, to understand the implicit and explicit demands imposed by the theme (Cain, 2018. p. 124; Elliott, 1991). Teacher voice is essential to this process and must establish the centrality of the theme to teachers and their classroom practice.

Research suggests the need to consider the vision of schools as professional learning organisations that can facilitate and support teachers' learning (Admiraal et al., 2019). The sense of belonging and collaborative achievement at the post-cycle dissemination event (the Teaching and Learning Conference commencing in Cycle 5) contributed to seeing research activity as an organic and integral part of a teacher's professional role. The conference provided a space for expressing professional pride in effective engagement with research, as well as opportunities to foster a 'cross-flow' of ideas between themselves and visiting stakeholders. The occasion provided an ideal moment to introduce university colleagues as part of the planned future partnership. The partnership was understood as 'externally supported expertise' and aimed to quality-assure the school's model for teacher-research (Godfrey, 2016, p. 313).

Conclusion

Rumworth School is projected to grow further, requiring effective strategic planning to prepare for this challenge. We propose that the implementation of whole-school teacher-led research provides an effective answer to the organisation of professional learning in this evolving environment. The democratic, teacher-led research model aligns organically with teacher professional practice and their rich, fluid and diverse situated practitioner knowledge. A community approach to continuous professional learning has therefore become a core value of Rumworth School, where wisdom sharing and a collegial professional development culture has transformed professional learning, mirroring the school's mission statement: 'You can do it; **we** will help'.

Response to the Editorial Perspective

Dana (2016, p. 1) suggests that practitioner research is 'shaped and reshaped in relation to the era within which it has existed' and therefore, must adapt reflexively to periods of educational change. We call attention to the fast expansion of SEND and alternative education, where two thirds of special schools, such as Rumworth, are at, or over, capacity (DfE, 2024a; National Audit Office, 2019). Practitioner research emerged as an answer to the challenges of expanding staff and student cohorts and the diversification of needs within the classroom. This model of professional learning served to expose teachers' diverse, contextual 'know-how' and provided a space where they could collectively articulate, and respond to, questions of practice.

References

Admiraal, W., Schenke, W., De Jong, L., Emmelot, Y., & Sligte, H. (2019). Schools as professional learning communities: What can schools do to support professional development of their teachers? *Professional Development in Education*, 47(4), 684–698. https://doi-org.ezproxy.bolton.ac.uk/10.1080/19415257.2019.1665573

Bokhove, C., & Hyde, R. (2024). Criticality in evidenced informed teaching: Expansive learning with Rosenshine. *Embedding a culture of Research in Schools. Impact Journal of the Chartered college of teaching*, (22). https://mhttps://my.chartered.college/impact_article/criticality-in-evidence-informed-teaching-expansive-learning-with-rosenshine/

Cain, T. (2018). *Becoming a research-informed school: Why? What? How?* Routledge.

Dana, N. F. (2016). The relevancy and importance of practitioner research in contemporary times. *Journal of Practitioner Research*, 1(1), 1–7.

de Paor, C., & Murphy, T. R. N. (2018). Teachers' views on research as a model of CPD: Implications for policy. *European Journal of Teacher Education*, 41(2), 169–186. https://doi.org/10.1080/02619768.2017.1416086

Department for Education (DfE). (2011). *Teachers standards*. Retrieved March 6, 2024, from https://www.gov.uk/government/publications/teachers-standards

Department for Education (DfE). (2016). *Educational excellence everywhere*. https://assets.publishing.service.gov.uk/media/5a804face5274a2e8ab4f6b7/Educational_Excellence_Everywhere.pdf

Department for Education (DfE). (2024a). *School capacity*. https://explore-education-statistics.service.gov.uk/find-statistics/school-capacity Accessed 25th April

Department for Education (DfE). (2024b). *Press Release: Government expands support for learners with SEND*. https://www.gov.uk/government/news/government-expands-support-for-pupils-with-send

Elliott, J. (1991). *Action research for educational change*. Milton Keynes, Open University Press.

Godfrey, D. (2016). Leadership of schools as research-led organisations in the English educational environment: Cultivating a research-engaged school culture. *Educational Management, Administration & Leadership*, 44(2), 301–321. https://doi.org/10.1177/1741143213508294

Guldberg, K., Parsons, S., Porayska-Pomsta, K., & Keay-Bright, W. (2017). Challenging the knowledge-transfer orthodoxy: Knowledge co-construction in technology-enhanced learning for children with autism. *British Educational Research Journal*, 43(2), 394–413. https://doi.org/10.1002/berj.3275

Kallitsoglou, A., & Mahmud, A. (2023). Teacher attitudes towards evidence-based practices for social, emotional and mental health difficulties in school and association with teacher academic research engagement. *Emotional and Behavioural Difficulties*, 28(4), 263–281. https://doi.org/10.1080/13632752.2023.2276024

Kennedy, A. (2005). Models of continuing professional development: A framework for analysis. *Journal of in-Service Education*, 31, 235–250. https://doi.org/10.1080/13674580500200277

Mandouit, L., & Hattie, J. (2023). Revisiting "The power of feedback" from the perspective of the learner. *Learning and Instruction*, 84, 101718. https://doi.org/10.1016/j.learninstruc.2022.101718

Müller, L., & Cook, V. (2024). Setting research priorities for applied cognitive sciences – What do teachers want from research? *British Educational Research Journal*, 50(3), 1471–1494. https://doi.org/10.1002/berj.3983

National Audit Office. (2019). *Support for pupils with special educational needs and disabilities in England: Report by the Controller and Auditor General (Full report)*. https://www.nao.org.uk/wp-content/uploads/2019/09/Support-for-pupils-with-special-education-needs.pdf

Office for National Statistics. (2022). *Educational experiences of young people with special educational needs and disabilities in England*. Data and Analysis from Census 2021. https://www.ons.gov.uk/peoplepopulationandcommunity/educationandchildcare/bulletins/educationalexperiencesofyoungpeoplewithspecialeducationalneedsanddisabilitiesinengland/februarytomay2022

Ovenden-Hope, T. (2024). From the Editor. Embedding a culture of Research in Schools. *Impact Journal of the Chartered College of Teaching*, (22). https://my.chartered.college/impact_article/from-the-editor-9/

Rosenshine, B. (2012). American educator. *American Federation of Teachers*, 36(1). https://www.aft.org/sites/default/files/Rosenshine.pdf

Sherrington, T. (2019). *Rosenshine's principles in action*. John Catt Educational. https://search.ebscohost.com/login.aspx?direct=true&scope=site&db=nlebk&db=nlabk&AN=2548550

Stenhouse, L. (1975). *An introduction to curriculum research and development*. Heinemann.

Stoll, L. (2015). *Three greats for a self-improving school system: Pedagogy, professional development and leadership: Executive summary*. Teaching schools R&D network national themes project 2012–14. Department for Education. assets.publishing.service.gov.uk/government/uploads/system/uploads/attachment_data/file/406279/Three_greats_for_a_self_improving_system_pedagogy_professional_development_and_leadership_executive_summary.pdf

Wilson, E. (2012) Introduction: Why should teachers do school based research? In E. Wilson (Ed.) School based research: *A guide for Education Students*. Sage Publications Ltd.

CHAPTER 10

Developing Research-Informed Trainee Teachers

Elizabeth Hidson
University of Sunderland, UK

ABSTRACT

This chapter explores the importance of developing practitioner research skills in trainee teachers. It argues that engaging trainee teachers in research at the micro (classroom) and meso (school) levels cultivates a questioning approach and research literacy. This prepares them to make evidence-informed decisions and contribute to a self-improving education system. Fostering a practitioner researcher identity in teachers bridges the gap between theory and practice, enabling them to apply research findings contextually and develop their teaching.

Keywords: Situational verification; reflective practice; questioning; action research; teacher agency; phronesis

Introduction: Learning to Teach

Learning to teach is a complex, nuanced process, with teaching variously described as an art, a science, a craft, a performance, or all of these. Biesta (2023) argued for an understanding of teaching that 'makes sense' and provides 'meaningful language' for teachers, linking this to Stenhouse's (1983) point that the desire to improve teaching is like that of the artist wanting to improve their craft. Stenhouse, of course, is invariably linked to the idea of the 'teacher as researcher'. Teaching teachers to teach, therefore, must draw in research to help them to understand what they are doing and why, and instil an aim to improve their artistry.

Stenhouse made the point that providing teachers with research findings and illustrative cases, although 'highly instructive' and useful for understanding, is still hypothetical knowledge in the form of principles and theories, in need of careful situational testing. Stenhouse further argues the point for teachers to treat the 'knowledge of their situation as capable of extension by systematic inquiry' (1983, p. 212), i.e. that they can learn by careful application of research findings in their own contexts. This is fertile ground for teacher educators: principles and theories can be explained to trainee teachers with the expectation that deeper understanding can be gained through 'situational verification'.

Discussion: Situational Verification by Trainee Teachers

Despite an increasing wealth of research evidence, it is widely reported that schools and teachers do not put this evidence to use to make informed decisions (Gorard et al., 2020; Pegram et al., 2022). Gorard et al. (2020) further suggest that clearer guidance and modelling on the use of research evidence is needed to improve the situation, and that involving users in research may also be fruitful. The central premise of this chapter is therefore that, if we are to develop practitioner researchers with sufficient knowledge, skills and understanding to contribute to a self-improving education system, we need to start as early as possible – while they are undertaking initial teacher training.

Those of us involved in teacher training encourage reflective practice and incremental improvements in the effectiveness of teaching. We set targets with trainee teachers based on their lesson observations and discussion of how they are planning and assessing the learning of their students. We support them to gather evidence of impact by gauging student responses to questioning, to evaluate lesson outputs as proxies for learning, and to employ formative and summative assessment strategies to help plan adaptations and next steps. In parallel, most teacher training involves some form of systematic review of practice, often in the form of a piece of applied or action research. Courses that include postgraduate-level assignments will usually link this formally to research and expect engagement with literature and research methods so that the trainee teacher can apply theory to practice. We task them to find 'best bets' from research and try it out for themselves. This is the embodiment of Stenhouse's 'situational verification'.

While teacher training must necessarily begin with the trainee, it is important that they see themselves as part of an interconnected education ecosystem to understand and differentiate practice at individual classroom or teacher level (micro), department or school level (meso) or wider structural and policy level (macro). The course that I teach focuses on trainees' initial research engagement on the meso level – trainees are asked to select and explore a school-based intervention to understand how and to what extent the institution's decision makers engage with research evidence. Using a case study approach, trainees observe, interview and collect school level data used to evaluate the intervention, and in so doing, develop a questioning approach to provision.

> **SCHOOL-BASED INTERVENTIONS**
>
> Amal, a trainee primary school teacher, explored a targeted maths intervention led by learning support assistants taking place each week during homework lessons held at the end of the day in her school. She read around the topic area and interventions, sat in to observe sessions and followed up with the staff leading the intervention to understand what progress was being made during the sessions. Not only did she develop a good understanding of the intervention and the skills needed to run the intervention, but by sharing her findings about the timing and frequency of the intervention with her colleagues, she was able to impact on future practice in the school.

Once trainees have learned essential approaches to research and evaluation at the meso level, they are then introduced to action research in the form of a negotiated individual study. At this micro level, they are tasked with using developmental or pedagogical goals as a starting point; they devise a research question, use an action research model to plan their cycles, analyse emerging classroom data, and reflect systematically on the process. We encourage them to take the Institute for Effective Education evaluation questions as their prompt – 'what impact does [what practice] delivered over [over how long] have on [what outcome?] for [whom?]' (Shaw, 2020, p. 7), with the supplemental, all-important 'and how do you know?' This challenges trainees, in line with McNiff (2017), to be able to make a knowledge claim that they have improved their practice, they can describe what they have done and explain why.

INDIVIDUAL ACTION RESEARCH

Ben trialled a rewards-based behaviour system in a Year 1 primary classroom. These pupils had mostly experienced online classes because of the COVID-19 pandemic, leading to a minimal foundation of expected classroom behaviour from their short time experiencing face-to-face classes in kindergarten. Through the action research project, it became clear to Ben that as more positive reinforcement was used, pupils responded better. This also appeared to yield more continuity of positive behaviour, particularly amongst pupils displaying low-level disruptive behaviour. Ben reviewed various approaches in his literature search, and was able to design suitable data collection methods and involve his mentor to support the project. Ben reflected on what he found, recognised limitations, and discussed the value of conducting further action research in individual classrooms with a view to developing policy at the school level.

> The value of developing research skills in trainee teachers is that they can then join the profession as early career teachers with a set of skills and a questioning approach from having been actively involved in research. They can take appropriate steps to impact on practice at the micro and meso level. If the ultimate aim is for schools to become better at making research-informed decisions, they need practitioners capable of systematically putting evidence to use for self-improvement.

Conclusion

Historically, it feels like there was something of a gap in relation to teachers as researchers around the turn of the century following on from thinkers such as Stenhouse and Shulman's arguments for a conception of teacher knowledge, agency and empowerment. The more recent focus on evidence-based education and evaluation seems to have opened the door again, albeit as part of a somewhat dichotomous debate about 'gold standard' research and randomised controlled trial (RCT) applicability (Nevill, 2019) versus local insights and asking 'what works for whom?' Thinking critically and carefully about researchable questions, research designs and situational variation does not need to exclude teachers, but the way that research is often framed as existing at the macro level of the ecosystem can seem exclusionary. Somewhere in between the mindset of researchers doing research and teachers doing teaching, is the realm of the practitioner researcher, who is invested in both.

I have previously maintained (Hidson, 2023) that the more teachers at all levels can embrace a practitioner researcher identity, the more the profession can focus collectively on identifying and addressing the gaps in our knowledge. This needs research literacy and a questioning approach to seeing what works in each classroom, school and region, anywhere in the world. Trainee teachers are exposed to research to inform their pedagogical development, influence curriculum planning and empower them to adapt their teaching to support their students.

As well as the skills, they need the agency and encouragement for purposeful action in their schools and classrooms.

Response to the Editorial Perspective

There is, at times, a risk of seeing teaching as a purely practical endeavour. In their editorial perspective piece, the editors of this book present practitioner research as having an affinity to pragmatism, but also as enabling the most appropriate choice for the practical problem in focus. I would like to extend this further by offering Eisner's (2002) application of the Greek term phronesis, a form of wise, practical reasoning, to teaching, summed up in this quote:

> *Practical reasoning is deliberative, it takes into account local circumstances, it weighs tradeoffs, it is riddled with uncertainties, it depends upon judgement, profits from wisdom, addresses particulars, it deals with contingencies, is iterative and shifts aims in process when necessary.* (Eisner, 2002, p. 375)

Eisner argues that while practical wisdom is valuable, it's not sufficient for excellence in teaching. He looks to make the transition from theoretical knowledge to practical wisdom in a similar way to Stenhouse. For trainee teachers, learning to reflect and deliberate as part of professional growth in the school environment is important for making the context-specific decisions needed for effective teaching. We as teachers, teacher educators, and practitioner researchers, recognise the value of learning through experience. While some forms of research may be capable of answering questions that can be generalised because of statistical significance, Eisner (and Stenhouse) help us to appreciate the value of contextualisation. This is how practitioner research can help trainee teachers to bridge the gap between seeing teaching as a science or an art: the practical application of theory allows for the immediate, in-flight decisions and actions that can always be refined as they develop their artistry.

Bringing this back to the editors' perspective, I align with their vision of practitioners as both consumers and producers of knowledge. However, from my position as a teacher educator I recognise the need to scaffold my trainees' experiences before they can fully embrace diverse research traditions. Trainees face significant challenges in transforming experts' tacit knowledge into codified and actionable knowledge. The focus on phronesis offered in this chapter serves as a vital staging post on the journey towards the 'methodologically sound, and personally and professionally meaningful' research envisioned by the editors. By positioning trainee teachers as future agents in a self-improving education ecosystem, we create a conceptual space where reflexivity for research-informed practice can be nurtured from its earliest stages.

References

Biesta, G. (2023). Reclaiming the artistry of teaching. In R. J. Tierney, F. Rizvi, & K. Ercikan (Eds.), *International encyclopedia of education* (4th ed., pp. 648–654). Elsevier. https://doi.org/10.1016/B978-0-12-818630-5.04034-3

Eisner, E. W. (2002). From episteme to phronesis to artistry in the study and improvement of teaching. *Teaching and Teacher Education*, *18*(4), 375–385. https://doi.org/10.1016/S0742-051X(02)00004-5

Gorard, S., See, B. H., & Siddiqui, N. (2020). What is the evidence on the best way to get evidence into use in education? *Review of Education*, *8*(2), 570–610. https://doi.org/10.1002/rev3.3200

Hidson, E. (2023). Research-informed teacher development: Perspectives from international initial teacher training. *Research Intelligence*, *155*, 26–27. https://www.bera.ac.uk/publication/summer-2023

McNiff, J. (2017). *Action research: All you need to know*. SAGE Publications.

Nevill, C. (2019, October 31). Randomised controlled trials – 3 good things, 3 bad things, and 5 top tips. *EEF Blog*. https://educationendowmentfoundation.org.uk/news/eef-blog-randomised-controlled-trials-or-how-to-train-your-dragon

Pegram, J., Watkins, R. C., Hoerger, M., & Hughes, J. C. (2022). Assessing the range and evidence-base of interventions in a cluster of schools. *Review of Education*, *10*, e3336. https://doi.org/10.1002/rev3.3336

Shaw, A. (2020). *Evaluation handbook*. Institute for Effective Education (IEE): York.

Stenhouse, L. (1983). The relevance of practice to theory. *Theory into Practice*, *22*(3), 211–215. https://doi.org/10.1080/00405848309543063

CHAPTER 11

Disrupting to Develop

Debbie Bogard, Freya Cox-Willmott and Neil Hart
City and Islington Sixth Form College, UK

ABSTRACT

A case study of how a distributed leadership model within a community of practice can foster professional growth and disrupt traditional hierarchies in education. By modelling and supporting reflective inquiry, and building outward-facing links across and beyond institutional spaces, the Teaching and Learning Community (TLC) serves as a powerful example of practitioner research that embraces an inclusive and inquisitive developmental approach to learning and sharing.

Keywords: Communities of practice; teaching and learning communities; mutual reciprocity; collective autonomy; collaborative learning; distributive leadership

Introduction

As colleagues in a relatively liberal Sixth Form College, we have been privileged with the opportunity to disrupt some of the discursive structures that have come to dominate schools and colleges. We have taken opportunities to collaborate, to give space for discussion and co-learning with students, to take actions to distribute power evenly within the classroom and within the institution. We have achieved this through reimagining our professional identities, growing rhizomatically (Deleuze & Guattari, 1980; Fox & Aldred, 2015) through links to other institutions, and collaborating on professional development projects built around our needs, and that are able to respond to the needs of our students.

During the pandemic, we rejuvenated our TLC, a community of practice that moves knowledge away from established silos and disrupts the status quo of learning within curricular settings, leading to a higher degree of cross-curricular cohesion and collaboration. Our TLC promotes a distributive, collective leadership model that encourages us to become active, agentic and self-directed in our learning and development (Bogard, Hart & Hughes, 2022). The fact that our community is peer-led and doesn't sit within established hierarchical structures with expected trajectories gives us space to think, learn and grow, taking us and our work to unexpected places.

Discussion

As our work as practitioner-researchers develops, the fundamental role collaboration and community building plays in the formation of our professional identities becomes startlingly clear. Our professional identities are relational, formed in collaboration with others. Inside the classroom, it takes the form of collaboration with colleagues, between teachers and students, and between students and students. Beyond the classroom, there are multiple interactions with other adults, including librarians, youth workers, catering and cleaning staff; all those who interact with students in the college space are educators.

In all of these sites of learning, the message is clear: collaboration is essential for disrupting hierarchies of power and community building. It is at the heart of what we do as educators who share the values and vision of bell hooks as education being the practice of freedom and centres of education being places of freedom, exploration, self-discovery, and relationship building (hooks, 1994). Increasingly, peer relationships develop within, between and beyond classrooms and institutions that question, challenge and subvert established norms and roles relating to title, rank and status.

In its place, we offer a different way of thinking and being in the classroom space; this commitment to a shared focus on our human qualities is imbued with radical potential. Like professional identities, power is a relational identity. It can be between two people, or groups, and is maintained through hierarchical structures. We disrupt those structures when we recognise that there is no hierarchy of knowledge, academic or experiential, when we value students' knowledge and experience as equally as theory, and when we work together to co-construct meaning and understanding.

Hierarchies of power are further disrupted when teachers and students are empowered to become researchers themselves. Within our TLC, our growing research focus has contributed to our own professional development and that of our colleagues and students, through the sharing of skills, knowledge and experiences. To illustrate, over the last three years, we have developed academic collaborations with research-practitioners in HE institutions, helping to make the classroom the locus of power. These collaborations have sought to affirm Stenhouse's values for effective practitioner-research partnerships, with teachers being intimately involved in the research process (Mills et al., 2000; Stenhouse, 1981). One current project has been developed through our TLC, working with a former colleague now working in teacher education. This shift from insider to outsider status, combined with the pre-existing trusting relationship based on shared values, has helped define and expand our third space between the academy and the classroom.

The project, Talking to Learn, focuses on the concept of 'expressive talk' (Barnes et al., 1974), the kind of talk that happens between students when teachers are out of earshot, with a view to understanding how meaning is made through these interactions. Being given the space and time to talk on their own terms, without a teacher guiding or interrupting the discourse, can help liberate students' thinking. Students can explore ideas in a way that is meaningful for them, becoming experts in their own talk, drawing on their own lives and experiences as a way of connecting with and navigating their subjects on their own terms (Bolton, 2009; Hippisley, 2020).

Another research project, Writing to Learn, was developed between our TLC and research-practitioners from Goldsmiths University. Working together across our shared sites of learning, our TLC were taught the principles of freewriting - writing automatically for a set period of time (Elbow, 1998) and diagrarting - a neologism of diagrams, dialogue and art (Gilbert, 2022), and were encouraged to reflect on our own practice and professional needs. This is a crucial part of the methodology, so that teachers bring their own experience and passion to the writing experience in order to model it in the classroom effectively (Bogard et al., 2023).

Having the opportunity to work in a creative collaboration within a mutually supportive and reciprocal relationship empowered us as teachers to develop this project, incorporating writing to learn into a range of subject areas drawing on our developing expertise. This work has helped us to shift the role of writing within our classrooms away from a high-stakes, performative activity towards something more connected to learning and thinking. Beyond our institution, we have shared our work through presenting at conferences and in publications. This has allowed us to share our professional learning and skills through connections with wider research communities and educator networks.

Within and beyond workplaces, communities of practice expand and develop through educator networks driven by practitioner-researchers committed to the sharing and disseminating of ideas, such as the Knowledge is Power curriculum at BSix Sixth Form College and the Connected Sociologies Curriculum Project (2024). It is here in this inclusive summer school that connections are made and opportunities are created between a diverse range of educators: academics, writers, poets, activists, youth workers, teachers and students. The seeds planted in such places germinate and unfurl in term time, spreading through our respective institutions, manifesting in research exchanges and enrichment programmes. Students pack out classrooms after hours, occupying intellectual spaces that are missing from the mainstream curriculum, where their own experiential ways of learning and thinking are validated and expanded.

In this third space, interactions change and hierarchies of teacher/student relationships are disrupted. We see how young people are co-creators of collective meaning when teachers aren't extracting specific answers from them, asking instead for their reflections, thoughts and ideas. This disrupts the idea that some knowledge has more value than that of the students, while simultaneously developing their ability to engage critically with what is being offered to them within the confines of the curriculum. In this way, they blur the arbitrary boundaries of curriculum knowledge/lived experience/habits of being and become active agents in their own learning, subverting the mind/body split that hooks warns us against (hooks, 1994).

In these spaces, we show ourselves as people rather than traditional and expected roles of teacher and student, and demonstrate the expansive, encompassing nature of our professional identities. Through not soliciting specific answers or interactions, we break out of the exchange economy of the classroom. Bell hooks stresses the importance of self-actualisation, the bringing together of mind, body and soul, reminding us that learning and knowledge are felt, not just thought (hooks, 2000).

Conclusion and Response to the Editorial Perspective

The editors point out in their Perspective of Practitioner Research that when inquiry becomes sustained, self-critical, systematic and/or shared, we can say it starts to take the form of research (Stenhouse, 1981). The highly academised educational landscape limits such opportunities for sustained and self-critical enquiry for many teachers. This is an environment that upholds and reinforces the separation of management from teachers and teachers from learners. Learning happens in discrete rooms and behind closed doors, with the teacher occupying the role of knowledge source, often working from materials designed centrally and delivered consistently to equalise the student experience.

As a group of teachers, we have found ways within our institution to establish, and co-construct, a third space between classroom practice and academic knowledge production where self-critical and shared enquiry has begun to develop into research. This third space has offered us a location of freedom from the discursive parameters of both the classroom and the university, where we have been able to enjoy constructing a hybrid teacher-researcher identity through building and sustaining connections with each other, with the students, and with other educational institutions, and playfully building new roles for ourselves. It gives us confidence to skilfully navigate and guide ourselves and our students away from data-driven, performance-oriented outcomes that undermine learning and towards richer and meaningful educational experiences. It has become an agentic, relational way of learning rooted in collective autonomy, drawing on our own and each other's experiences as a way to expand and deepen our thinking and questioning.

In a diverse and politically engaged community of teachers and students, transgression and disruption of dominant norms are explained with reference to bell hooks' work on education as the practice of freedom rather than a tool of domination. By dismantling the hierarchies that exist in the classroom, we work to prevent classrooms from becoming places that reproduce systems of domination. The work of our TLC is defined by praxis and an implementation of our educational values: everything that we ask the students to do we trial with ourselves in the spirit of mutual reciprocity. We work to open our minds, to engage in rigorous study, to think critically and to disseminate and disrupt power in the classroom and the institution: a union between theory and praxis.

It is our hope that this case study has significance beyond our institution through its representation of a widespread shift in the culture of educational establishments. Through the sharing of experiences, we seek to offer support for teachers who feel disempowered within their own educational institutions, aiming to empower teachers to shape their own professional identities. Modelling the connections between teachers beyond the boundaries of their institutions aims to provide a model for rhizomatic growth of networks of professional practice that allow teachers to regain power in a political context through creating and cultivating communities of practice as resistance.

Acknowledgements

The authors would like to thank Connected Sociologies, Knowledge is Power, Su Hippisley and Francis Gilbert for creating safe spaces to explore, engage and challenge dominant narratives in education. Thank you for showing us what genuine collaboration looks and feels like. Thank you also to Anna Douglas who created our TLC in 2010, and for her ongoing mentorship and guidance.

And to all our students who we learn from everyday.

References

Barnes, B., Britton, J., & Rosen, H. (1974). *Language, the learner and the school*. Penguin.

Bogard, D. (2023). Teaching and Learning Communities as a vehicle for developing action research. *Bera blog*. Retrieved June 23, 2024, from https://www.bera.ac.uk/blog/teaching-and-learning-communities-as-a-vehicle-for-developing-action-research

Bogard, D., Gilbert, F., Hart, N., & Hughes, S. (2023). The teacher as researcher: Collaborative research in further education. *Research Intelligence*, 155, 21.

Bogard, D., Hart, N., & Hughes, S. (2022). Teacher driven CPDL: A teaching and learning community in action. *Impact*, 15. Retrieved April 27, 24, from chartered.college

Bolton, G. (2009). Write to learn: Reflective practice writing. *InnovAiT*, 2(12), 752–754.

Deleuze, G., & Guattari, F. (1980). *A thousand plateaus*. Bloomsbury Academic.

Elbow, P. (1998). *Writing without teachers*. Oxford University Press.

Fox, N., & Aldred, P. (2015). Inside the research-assemblage: New materialism and the micropolitics of social inquiry. *Sociological Research Online*, 20(2), 6.

Gilbert, F. (2022). Diagrarting: Theorising and practicing new ways of writing. *New Writing*, 19(2), 153–182.

Hippisley, S. (2020). Unearthing forbidden stratagems: Talk, transgression and reading The Duchess of Malfi. *Changing English*, 27(4), 408–418.

hooks, b. (1994). *Teaching to transgress: Education as the practice of freedom*. Routledge.

hooks, b. (2000). *All about love: New visions*. William Morris.

Mills, M., Mockler, N., Stacey, M., & Taylor, B. (2020). Teachers' orientations to educational research and data in England and Australia: Implications for teacher professionalism. *Teaching Education*, *32*(2), 1–22.

Stenhouse, L. (1981). What counts as research? *British Journal of Educational Studies, 29*(2), 103–114. https://doi.org/10.1080/00071005.1981.9973589

The Connected Sociologies Curriculum Project. (2024). Retrieved from September 16, 2025 from https://thesociologicalreview.org/announcements/news/connected-sociologies-curriculum-project-completion/

CHAPTER 12

Developing Professional Knowledge as a Consortium: Moving from 'I' to 'We'[1]

The RATED Consortium Consisting of:
Claire Haresnape Tyson[a],
Matthew J. Easterbrook[b], Lewis Doyle[b],
Alison Glover[c], Elizabeth Hidson[d]
and Thomas Perry[e]

[a]Homewood School and Sixth Form Centre
[b]University of Sussex
[c]The Open University
[d]University of Sunderland
[e]University of Warwick

ABSTRACT

Spoken by a teacher researcher from the 'third space', this chapter explores a practical solution to a school-based problem. Claire Tyson explains how, as consortium members, they explored their shared values and theories as well as harnessing their differences, to create a consortium focused on a project about unconscious teacher bias. Learning, as they did so, that maintaining strong lines of communication, having complementary perceptions of the impact of the consortium and shared motivations for participation were important factors. By bringing together both practical and academic forms of knowledge, they showed a willingness to embrace the multiple perspectives represented in the group.

Keywords: Third space; practitioner research; research-practice partnerships; collaboration; teacher bias

Introduction

> As a teacher researcher in a secondary school I sit in the 'third space' (Skattebol & Arthur, 2014, p. 363), a sometimes uncomfortable and uneasy position due to the contested nature of the relationship between educational research and educational practice. (Biesta & Aldridge, 2021, p. 1449) – Claire

In this contribution, we explore a practical solution to this problem, explaining how we forged an alliance with researchers from Higher Education, how we navigate our differences in background and role, and describing our first shared project on tackling unconscious teacher bias. We draw upon our shared values, which are in line with a pragmatist worldview, our shared understanding of Close-to-Practice Research (Parsons, 2021), our own domains of expertise and an appreciation of the practical wisdom that underpins good teacher practice. Although we have not formally characterised ourselves as an Education Research-Practice Partnership, we do share many of their characteristics as described by Wentworth et al. (2024). Maintaining strong lines of communication, having complementary perceptions of the impact of our consortium and shared motivations for participation that relate to our larger goals are all evident when we reflect on our progress to date.

Discussion: Coalescence

The origins of the RATED consortium can be traced back to contacts created in an earlier research project. The opportunity to participate in the EEF 'Writing about Values' project in 2016/2017 (See et al., 2018), brought our school into contact with Dr Matthew Easterbrook and his team at the University of Sussex, School of Psychology. Over the course of the next five years, we planned and delivered an iteration of Writing about Values at Homewood School Sixth Form and this intervention is now embedded into our KS5 Pastoral Programme.

Despite the challenges of school closures during the COVID-19 pandemic, Matthew and I managed to maintain a commitment to working together. This included meeting in person as well as the increasing use of virtual meetings, particularly in the post-pandemic landscape. The benefits of being involved in a school gave Matt and his associates a connection with the grounded reality of classroom practice, whereas I benefited from being able to access his academic expertise and ethics panel resources. Moving from being participants in 'their trial' to becoming research partners, shifted the power dynamics to create a more equal relationship. The developing connection also gave credibility to my role as a teacher researcher by demonstrating to my school that I was creating genuine outward facing relationships that brought benefit to the school.

A new challenge arose when my school became aware that a group of parents were not engaging with the school's parent consultation appointments. Building on our work with Matthew about 'Stereotype anxiety' (Morris, Gorard, & Siddiqui, 2018), I was interested in exploring this data further but I was conscious that it was potentially sensitive data and a high stakes exercise so I felt that some external research support might be a good idea. I approached academic consultants who specialised in this field but it was clear that this was not an affordable option for our school. At the same time, I was becoming aware of debates about the nature of 'expert knowledge' and 'Close to Practise' research, and realising that we were not necessarily in a position of weakness. We could draw upon our own knowledge and skills if we collaborated with the right partners.

The existing relationship with the University of Sussex was a robust starting point, and other connections had been made through my work as a co-convenor for the BERA Practitioner Research SIG. AF from the Open University was an important influence who gave me the confidence to reach out via email to my network. My timing was perfect, a growing interest in working with schools led to four academics responding to my callout. In early June 2022, I was able to hold an online scoping meeting attended by myself, Thomas Perry, A H-J, Carmel Capewell and Matthew Easterbrook. The 'I' had become 'we'.

Our group has not been static, the sad loss of A H-Jl in 2023 was acknowledged by the Open University who were keen to honour her academic legacy and suggested that Alison Glover would be a good fit for our group. We have also welcomed Elizabeth Hidson and Lewis Doyle, research assistant CG, and more recently post-graduate student A-F C-M.

Although we have different backgrounds (teaching economics, sociology, child development, teacher education and psychology), we have a common interest in tackling educational disadvantages. This fitted well with the intersectional issues on which the group has focused: our starting point for understanding educational inequalities was that there are many reasons why some groups of students can have lower performance, attendance, and poorer behaviour records and these include structural and psychological reasons.

We characterised ourselves as an informal group of close-to-practice academics, teachers, and teacher educators who collaboratively work together to reduce educational inequalities and disadvantages using evidence-based approaches. Thomas Perry was tasked with finding an acronym; his suggestion of RATED (Research-Informed Approaches to Tackling Educational Disadvantage) was agreed by the group. Our early virtual meetings were used for introductions and explorations of our intersecting interests, values and skills, the intersecting interest was a focus on inequality and narrowing the gaps that exist for students.

We identified unconscious teacher bias as a potential area for research and in September 2022 we first started working on co-developing a rubric tool for teachers to use in conjunction with video technology (https://www.schoolinclusion.org.uk/access-further-materials). Teacher bias against learners' social identities can have a significant impact on their educational experiences and outcomes (Childs & Wooten, 2023). Teacher bias on the basis of social class and 'race' in particular, are key reasons for inequity in education (Gillborn, 2015).

Although bias is a difficult topic to approach it does need to be tackled head on as it tends to perpetuate existing inequalities. We discussed the sensitive nature of bias in practice, looking at it from our different perspectives of academics or teachers, and how this can be framed for working in schools thus avoiding the 'Gotcha' or negative perception of practice.

There has been no 'blueprint' for working together but our shared values have helped create a group identity. Another thing that has gone in our favour was a successful funding application from Sussex University which allowed us to pay a research assistant to conduct a literature review and to coordinate a pilot study to co-create and design the rubric with teachers and students from Homewood School.

As a group we are interested in the idea of Phronesis (Biesta, 2007), and how the practical wisdom of great teaching is developed through both experience and ongoing learning. In the context of informed, practical action, we are conscious that the nature of educational issues is not always immediately clear and tend to be interconnected. Our analogy is that investigating educational inequalities is like moving to a new school – it takes time to make sense of the people and the context; understanding of the issues and possible responses emerges in connection with one's familiarisation with the new school rather than being something one can know in advance.

My role as a teacher researcher also enables the practical issues, such as the time and resources, to act as the administrator for the group. By using shared drives and virtual meetings that are not too long or too frequent, we have built an enjoyable working relationship based upon mutual respect. We have a flat power structure with responsibilities based on skill sets rather than a hierarchical structure.

Conclusion

There was always an assumption that both academic and practical forms of knowledge were important, connected and connectable. Keeping an ecosystem model in mind (Bronfenbrenner, 2005), the locus of the research questions and the way that these might be tackled have been co-constructed between the school and the RATED team. The issues are rooted in knowledge of the school, but are turned into a 'researchable' question through the collaboration. We are an example of both applied and applying education research, blending both academic and practice-led thinking.

We now acknowledge and celebrate our individual successes and support each other as a group with activities such as funding applications, writing for publication and conference submissions. At the time of writing this, we are working together to source more funding to allow us to continue developing our rubric project.

Response to the Editorial Perspective

What does Dewey's pragmatism have to offer us? Taking our rubric project as an example, the psychologists in the group used theory and evidence to design the rubric, but needed the pragmatic input from the teachers to find out whether it would work in practice. There is a form of knowledge that sits in psychology which represents/describes the world, and the consortium is taking that conceptual knowledge and converting it into pragmatic knowledge through action and inquiry. In this way, we create knowledge together by acting and reflecting on the results of those actions. We are essentially pluralistic in nature, acknowledging that the world is complex and multifaceted, and that we need to take multiple perspectives and put them together in order to explain it. Having a consortium with members with different ontological and epistemological positions facilitates this pluralistic position (Shan & Williamson, 2023).

Our different backgrounds allow us to bring different viewpoints and one consortium member described our discussions as a 'bridge' that translates knowledge from each of our domains and returns new, co-constructed knowledge to that domain. By avoiding our silos, we create richer ideas about how useful these concepts are both as theoretical frameworks and practical actions. We are open to being theoretically flexible, all forms of knowledge are valued and everybody has input as the project evolves. Our takeaway message is that a successful collaboration between practitioners and researchers must embrace this pluralism and the values that it represents.

Note

1. A few names in this chapter have been anonymised as AF, A H-J, CG, and A-F C-M.

References

Biesta, G. (2007). Why "what works" won't work: Evidence-based practice and the democratic deficit in educational research. *Educational Theory*, 57(1), 1–22.

Biesta, G., & Aldridge, D. (2021). The contested relationships between educational research, theory and practice: Introduction to a special section. *British educational research journal*, 47(6), 1447–1450.

Bronfenbrenner, U. (2005). *Ecological systems theory* (1992).

Childs, T. M., & Wooten, N. R. (2023). Teacher bias matters: An integrative review of correlates, mechanisms, and consequences. *Race Ethnicity and Education*, 26(3), 368–397.

Gillborn, D. (2015). Intersectionality, critical race theory, and the primacy of racism: Race, class, gender, and disability in education. *Qualitative Inquiry*, 21(3), 277–287.

Parsons, S. (2021). The importance of collaboration for knowledge co-construction in 'close-to-practice' research. *British Educational Research Journal*, 47(6), 1490–1499.

See, B. H., Morris, R., Gorard, S., & Siddiqui, N. (2018). Writing about values: Evaluation report and executive summary Education Endowment Fund. https://d2tic4wvo1iusb.cloudfront.net/production/documents/projects/Writing_About_Values_1.pdf?v=1757437266

Shan, Y., & Williamson, J. (2023). *Evidential pluralism in the social sciences* (p. 191). Taylor & Francis in the Social Sciences (Philosophy and Method in the Social Sciences).

Skattebol, J., & Arthur, L. M. (2014). Collaborative practitioner research: Opening a third space for local knowledge production. *Asia Pacific Journal of Education*, 34(3), 351–365.

Wentworth, L., Fox, L., & Reardon, S. F. (2024). Education research-practice partnerships: Impacts and dynamics. *Peabody Journal of Education*, 99(3), 314–329.

CHAPTER 13

An Insider Perspective: Exploring Teachers' Engagement with Professional Development in Cooperation with Practitioner Co-Researchers

Marianne Talbot
University of Leeds, UK

ABSTRACT

This chapter reflects on some of the findings of a Research England[1] funded project about how best to support teachers to overcome barriers to engage with professional development (PD). Teachers can find it difficult to take part in PD, due to a variety of factors, including but not limited to lack of finance, disruption to teaching and learning, difficulty of finding suitable supply cover, lack of awareness of opportunities, and unsupportive leaders or colleagues (Krille, 2020). The findings presented here suggest that money can help reduce barriers by paying for supply staff so that teachers can be released to take part in training, for example, but they also suggest that the support and backing of employers is a major factor in releasing teachers in 'school time' to access PD, which has additionally been affected in recent years by the diminished role of Local Authorities in providing training, the rise of Multi-Academy Trusts offering trust-specific opportunities, and the COVID-19 pandemic. The intentions of this project were to seek practitioners' involvement in understanding how barriers to PD can be overcome, and why and how PD works when it works, partly by showcasing strategies and models adopted by the researcher-practitioners themselves.

Keywords: Barriers; challenges; professional development; practitioners; strategies; models

Introduction

This chapter reports findings of a Research England funded project that I led as a postgraduate researcher in summer 2022, focusing on how teachers engage with PD and how best to support them to overcome barriers to engage with PD. The starting point for the research was a discussion with a colleague about teachers finding it difficult to take part in PD, linked to factors including lack of finance, disruption to teaching and learning, difficulty of finding suitable supply cover, lack of awareness of opportunities, and unsupportive leaders or colleagues (Krille, 2020). I believe that successful PD will embrace and encourage discussion and reflection, including permission to try ideas out in the classroom or staffroom, and to fail before succeeding. This echoes the work of Guskey (1986, 2000), which links PD to practice. My chosen methodology blended qualitative and collaborative approaches, based on surveys and roundtables with groups of participant-practitioners, a mixture of teachers plus other professionals working to support teacher PD.

Discussion

The Sample and Main Features of Successful PD

My research was based on working with a sample of 14 teachers and other education professionals who worked together to identify and evaluate the following features of successful, valued, and valuable PD:

- **high quality and accessible** – low cost or free and available at an appropriate time and via an appropriate mode of delivery

- **relevant to the individual,** including their career stage, teaching experience, responsibilities, and interests; everyone is unique and will have unique PD needs
- **relevant to the needs of the teacher's school,** which probably means that it must be directly linked to improving student outcomes
- **selected by teachers trusted to use their autonomy and agency** to choose appropriate PD from the range on offer, including observing or working with teachers who can model excellent skills, behaviours, and attitudes, or working with other schools, or being an examiner for an awarding organisation.

Methodology

Three online roundtable discussions, supported by pre- and post-event surveys, used a purposeful sampling approach whereby practising teacher participants were selected from volunteers who, despite the perceived barriers, had taken part in PD (Creswell & Plano Clarke, 2018). They also included other professionals involved in promoting teacher PD, such as union officials and subject/professional association staff, which fitted with the Research England theme of 'building a supportive and collegiate environment' (University of Leeds, 2022).

The purposes of the research were to identify barriers to PD, how participants overcame barriers, what motivated them to access PD, if or how they were supported (financially and otherwise) and by whom, and what they did once they had engaged in PD, concentrating on the impact of PD on participants, their influence on other colleagues, any sustained changes to practice, remaining challenges, and ongoing benefits. Participants were offered supply cover or a small fee to encourage engagement, because it was an important element of the research design to have the participants fully involved in the co-development of the roundtables, based on their survey responses.

The study was designed using a predominantly qualitative approach to data collection, using thematic analysis of survey responses and roundtable inputs, supplemented by quantitative analysis of the survey data. I drew on the work of Bryman (2001, p. 264) and Clark (2021, p. 351), building on the survey responses and input from the participant-practitioners to inform the initial roundtable prompts. Thereafter, the participants became co-constructors of the research (Lyndon & Edwards, 2022) as they contributed to the operation of the roundtables, introducing novel aspects of the discussions and probing each other about their PD experiences.

> **CASE STUDY A: LINKING THE PERSONAL WITH THE PROFESSIONAL (DARREN NORTHCOTT, NATIONAL OFFICIAL (EDUCATION), NASUWT: THE TEACHERS' UNION)**
>
> Feeling positive about PD as a teacher is important, both personally and professionally. We believe teacher ownership and commitment to PD is an important part of a successful approach to PD, along with, for example, PD being seen as part of the strategic work of the school. Where this happens, teachers tend to report a more positive PD experience. Another area where the personal and professional meet is the relationship between PD and performance management or appraisal. When discussing objectives, it is incumbent upon the manager to make sure the necessary support to meet this objective is provided. Done well in a non-punitive way that can be extremely powerful. What we see is that when teachers have a sense of agency, a sense in which they feel that they are co-authors of their PD journey, they are more positive about PD. What good schools and good employers do is make sure that their PD offer is purposeful professionally, and then it is meaningful personally and teachers are active participants in that process.

The pre-event survey elicited a small amount of data about participants' lengths and levels of experience as teachers or as professionals supporting teachers and established a general picture of their perspectives on access to and engagement with PD, which was used to help identify emerging themes for further investigation in the roundtables. A similar, post-event, survey captured views after the roundtables. The surveys were complemented by three, online, 2–2.5 hour roundtable discussions, held in MS Teams. The term 'roundtables' was used rather than focus groups deliberately to promote open, free-ranging, frank, democratic conversations, avoiding hierarchies or preconceived notions of the participants as 'research subjects' and encouraging exposure to, consideration of, and reaction to others' perspectives (Evans & Kotchetkova, 2009). Hence, the roundtables allowed participants to interact, react to, and challenge each other's contributions, via 'frank discussion and information sharing' and 'informal, discursive activity' (McAvinia & Oliver, 2004, pp. 212, 222), participating as co-researchers by introducing different concepts to the conversations.

Researcher Positionality

I take an insider position (Saidin & Yaacob, 2016), having been involved in teaching and PD of teachers for many years. Indeed, some of the participants had previously taken part in PD that I have led, so their positionality was also potentially compromised. As Fleming (2018) says, drawing a distinction between previous relationships between participants and researchers, especially when co-researching, is important. Corbin Dwyer and Buckle (2009, p. 59) suggest that 'disciplined bracketing and detailed reflection on the subjective research process, with a close awareness of one's own personal biases and perspectives' helps with this distinction, as can being 'open, authentic, honest, deeply interested in the experience of one's research participants, and committed to accurately and adequately representing their experience'. Mercer (2007, p. 1) proposes that 'the insider/outsider dichotomy is actually a continuum with multiple dimensions'. Hence, I remain hyper-aware of my positionality and potential biases, and those of my co-researchers, and continue to carefully mitigate them as far as possible, but by acknowledging and working with them, I believe they can enrich my research, rather than harm it.

> **CASE STUDY B: FLEXIBLE AND RICH PD OFFER (LISA-MARIA MÜLLER, HEAD OF RESEARCH AND POLICY, CHARTERED COLLEGE OF TEACHING)**
>
> We are seeing really positive engagement with live online webinars and with recorded versions, which build on the live session, and offer a flexible way for delegates to access PD. We encourage teachers to sign up for such PD even if they cannot attend a live webinar, as they will then have access to the recording and any associated resources, such as an interactive element that takes place after the webinar itself. For example, some webinars are combined with a Padlet where we encourage teachers to share additional resources, so it is there as a rich resource for teachers to go back to whenever they need to. We might also add reflection questions, additional reading, and additional resources pointing to, say, articles in our journal. In this way, by adding additional resources, we create bite-sized but rich online learning units based on some webinars, which takes the PD well beyond just the original webinar or recording. We have started to use many recordings in this more flexible way precisely to encourage engagement, where delegates can access a webinar as a podcast which they can listen to while they prepare dinner or do some gardening or whatever. All teachers are busy and tend to multitask!

Conclusion

The study identified key features of successful PD, based on a small sample of participants collaborating on the process and outcomes. To be of value and to overcome barriers such as lack of time and workload, PD must be relevant to the individual, including career stage, experience as a teacher, current or imminent responsibilities, and interests. The research recognises that everyone is unique and will have PD needs specific to them as an individual. PD must also be high quality and accessible, including low cost or free and available at an appropriate time and via an appropriate mode of delivery. For example, online courses (including recordings) can be made available whenever teachers prefer to access them.

As well as being personalised, PD must meet the needs of the teacher and their school, which probably means that it must be directly linked to improving student outcomes. Teachers should be trusted to use their autonomy and agency to choose appropriate PD, selecting from the range on offer. This might include observing or working with other successful teachers who can model excellent skills, behaviours, and attitudes. It also might include working with other schools and/or being an examiner for an awarding organisation, for example.

It seems essential to protect and allocate PD time for all teachers, and to assign time for sharing and embedding the learning arising from PD. Successful PD will always encourage discussion and include opportunities for reflection, including permission to try ideas out in the classroom or staffroom, linking PD to practice, and to fail before succeeding, which echoes the work of Guskey (1986, p. 6).

Response to the Editorial Perspective

The editors state that one aspect of Practitioner Research is to contribute to the PD of colleagues and students by sharing and fostering research skills and research knowledge.

This research was strengthened by the depth and breadth of knowledge of my willing co-researchers, who were keen to share their diverse experiences, supporting the idea that practitioner-researchers add value to research about their identity, agency, and practice, whilst also adding to their own expertise and enriching their practice. Whilst barriers remain to teachers desiring access to high-quality and relevant PD, there are workable solutions being used in many schools, and by carrying out collaborative practitioner research, those solutions can be discovered and shared, by researchers, their co-researchers, and by those interested to read about the research. Such real-world solutions fit with the philosophy, methodology, and ethics of the approach taken here and elsewhere in this book.

Note

1. Research England is responsible for funding and engaging with English higher education providers, to create and sustain the conditions for a healthy and dynamic research and knowledge exchange system in the higher education sector. See: https://www.ukri.org/councils/research-england/

References

Bryman, A. (2001). *Social research methods*. Oxford University Press.
Clark, T. (2021). *Bryman's social research methods* (6th ed.). Oxford University Press.
Corbin Dwyer, S., & Buckle, J. L. (2009). The space between: On being an insider-outsider in qualitative research. *International Journal of Qualitative Methods, 8*(1), 54–63.
Creswell, J. W., & Plano Clarke, V. L. (2018). *Designing and conducting mixed methods research* (3rd ed., International student edition). SAGE.
Evans, R., & Kotchetkova, I. (2009). Qualitative research and deliberative methods: Promise or peril? *Qualitative Research, 9*(5), 625–643.
Fleming, J. (2018). Recognizing and resolving the challenges of being an insider researcher in work-integrated learning. *International Journal of Work-Integrated Learning, Special Issue, 19*(3), 311–320.
Guskey, T. R. (1986). Staff development and the process of teacher change. *Educational Researcher, 15*(5), 5–12.
Guskey, T. R. (2000). *Evaluating professional development*. Corwin Press.

Krille, C. (2020). Barriers to participation in professional development. In *Teachers' participation in professional development*. Springer Briefs in Education. Springer. https://doi.org/10.1007/978-3-030-38844-7_4

Lyndon, S., & Edwards, B. (2022). Beyond listening: The value of co-research in the co-construction of narratives. *Qualitative Research*, 22(4), 613–631. https://doi.org/10.1177/1468794121999600

McAvinia, C., & Oliver, M. (2004). Developing a managed learning environment using 'roundtables': An activity theoretic perspective. *Interactive Learning Environments*, 12(3), 209–225.

Mercer, J. (2007). The challenges of insider research in educational institutions: Wielding a double-edged sword and resolving delicate dilemmas. *Oxford Review of Education*, 33(1), 1–17.

Saidin, K., & Yaacob, A. (2016). Insider researchers: Challenges & opportunities. 2016 *International Seminar on Generating Knowledge Through Research, UUM-UMSIDA, 25-27 October 2016, Universiti Utara Malaysia, Malaysia Conference Proceedings* (pp. 849–854). ICECRS. https://core.ac.uk/download/pdf/154353144.pdf

University of Leeds. (2022). *Research culture crucible*. https://researchersupport.leeds.ac.uk/research-culture/research-culture-crucible/

CHAPTER 14

The Research-Engaged Practitioner: The Importance of Research Literacy and Critical Reflection for the Novice Teacher's Professional Learning

Leanne Henderson[a], Danyah Alsayeud[b] and Ian Collen[a]

[a]Queen's University Belfast, UK
[b]University of Jeddah, Saudi Arabia

ABSTRACT

This contribution examines the role of Initial Teacher Education (ITE) in preparing novice teachers to embrace their identity as research-engaged practitioners. It argues that professional learning is built upon the cultivation of research literacy and critical self-reflection. The approach aligns with professional standards which place value on engagement with research evidence to develop, evaluate and reflect on practice. The authors discuss how the ITE student experience can be enhanced by flexible and inclusive pedagogy.

Keywords: Practitioner research; reflective practice; initial teacher education (ITE); research literacy; research-engaged practice

Introduction

The 21st-century teacher is a research-informed and research-engaged (Saunders, 2017) practitioner. National and school-level policies give priority to developing teaching practices which are informed by the best available evidence (Coldwell et al., 2017). Needless to say, the pace and volume of research activity and resulting evidence can be difficult to keep on top of. How then are we to equip students in our ITE programmes to navigate this complex but essential area of their professional practice? In our view, the ability to independently identify, access, interpret, and make use of research evidence is a crucial skill which contributes to a teacher's career-long learning.

In recognition of the clearly articulated prominence of reflective practice from the early career phase (GTCNI, 2011), we wish to emphasise the extent to which high-quality professional learning is built upon 'collaborative, critical and contextually relevant learning' (Pollard et al., 2023, p. 108). Thus, enabling novice teachers to engage in democratic professionalism (Sachs, 2001) to embrace 'the interconnectedness of transformative processes in inquiry, teaching, and learning' (Dusty, 2024, p. 165).

ITE in Support of Practitioner Research

We are a group of language education practitioners who bring our own views and experiences together in considering how best early career teachers can be equipped to engage with and develop their identity as a researcher. Our own backgrounds span classroom research from primary to university-levels and engaging in the practice of research has contributed positively to our identities as both teachers and researchers. These experiences, alongside our professional discussions and collaborations, have shaped our thinking, writing and teaching about what it means for practitioners to engage in research and inquiry.

Critical Reflective Practice

Equipping novice teachers to engage in critical reflective practice is crucial for their professional learning and growth.

Dewey's seminal work in defining reflective thought emphasises the importance of 'active, persistent, and careful consideration' of existing beliefs in light of supporting evidence (Dewey, 1933, p. 118). Schön (1987) emphasises the dual role of reflection '-in-action' (in the moment) and '-on-action' (with some retrospect) in contributing to continuous, experiential learning within professional practice.

While reflective practice encourages self-critical engagement, it is not necessarily, nor always, critical (Pollard et al., 2023). Teachers can develop proficiency in designing, evaluating, and revising successful learning experiences for their students without necessarily engaging their broader critical consciousness to any meaningful degree (Freire, 1970). However, reflective thought risks being incomplete if it ignores broader social and political influences and values. Mezirow's (1991) theory of transformative learning, alongside insights from Dewey and Schön, underscore the significance of intentionally and critically examining and reshaping assumptions, beliefs, and viewpoints. Through reflective practice, novice teachers can deepen their comprehension of teaching and learning, recognise biases, and cultivate more inclusive and effective teaching methodologies. Indeed, activating the critical dimension of reflection can positively and explicitly influence teacher autonomy and identity.

To support novice teachers in engaging with reflective practice, we have consistently employed Jay and Johnson's (2002) three-stage typology. Within this approach, students are asked to address three key areas: Descriptive, identifying the matter for reflection and establishing specific areas requiring additional thought; Comparative, considering the issue in light of personal experiences, peer perspectives, and research evidence; and Critical, bringing an evaluative and analytic lens to challenge assumptions and beliefs, arriving at a more informed and nuanced perspective. In addition to explicitly teaching this framework, students are required to engage in periodic self-reflective evaluations of their practice using this model. While challenging at first, students develop proficiency in reflective inquiry over time, accelerating their acquisition of the skills underpinning effective critical self-reflection.

Our renewed focus on independent identification, appraisal and application of research evidence contributes to how we frame the relationship between critical reflection and research-informed practice for our learners. Drawing on Farrell and Kennedy's (2019) framework, we re-emphasise the cyclical rather than linear nature of reflection and signpost the value of adopting a more flexible, multifaceted evaluation of practice. Ultimately, deeper self-discovery is rooted in a teacher's ability to connect their practice to their personal philosophies and principles. It is from this standpoint that practitioners are equipped to respond to and evaluate research evidence within their critical self-reflective practice.

Action Research to Extend Critical Self-Reflective Practice

Our teaching and assessment of research skills amongst ITE students have been for many years related to a discrete individual 'Action Research' project (Carr & Kemmis, 1986; Kemmis et al., 2014) with a view to building novice teachers' ability to engage in practitioner research and capacity to critique educational research (Stenhouse, 1985). This approach has served us and our graduates well in understanding how important questions about learning and teaching can be answered with depth, nuance, and immediacy by those with the greatest power to engage directly in the processes and practices of learning and teaching: classroom teachers.

The preferred approach, introduced, taught, and continually reviewed by staff for multiple successive cohorts, enabled emerging classroom practitioners to acquire skills in identifying areas of their practice which would benefit from additional detailed focus, developing an intervention or approach intended to improve that aspect of practice, testing out the approach before evaluating and reflecting upon its efficacy, will be familiar – perhaps second nature – to our practitioner researcher colleagues. Most recently, in elaborating the collaborative and transformative elements of our work, we were informed and supported by the *Action research communities for language teachers approach*, developed by Christine Lechner and colleagues (European Centre for Modern Languages of the

Council of Europe, n.d.). This framing enabled our ITE students, all modern languages specialists, to develop awareness of the international trend towards enhancing teacher autonomy and professionalism through critical reflection.

The (Unexpected) Evolution of the Novice Teacher's Research Role

As with Action Research, innovations in education often develop as a response to particular 'problems' which arise in the course of practice. During the lockdowns associated with the COVID-19 pandemic, our own practice as teacher educators required emergency adaptation to support our students to complete their individual projects to meet the relevant assessment objectives of their course. Given the substantial, unprecedented, and unpredictable nature of education delivery at all levels, we felt that the conduct of a desk-based study was the most suitable means to enable ITE students to develop their mindset as a researcher without requiring them to engage in classroom-based research activity.

All of the students had completed an extended school-based professional placement, and all were on placement during the lockdown. Of course, there were highly variable conditions for the lockdown placements, ranging from supporting the children of key workers in school to teaching remotely. We designed an 'alternative' assignment which required students to summarise and evaluate the research literature on a particular topic relevant to learning and teaching in modern languages and to provide a reflection on its relevance to their own practice. Our students, in the most difficult circumstances, produced well-informed and thoughtful assignments which gave insight into their capacity to engage meaningfully with research evidence and to apply this to think critically about practice.

Conclusion and Response to the Editorial Perspective

Reflecting on the philosophical worldview underpinning this volume, our position is that engaging in practice-based inquiry through Action Research remains a valuable element of a teacher's professional repertoire and a means by which teachers can develop, evaluate, and transform their practice. The Department of Education's (DE) (2016) *Learning Leaders* strategy highlights that all teachers are 'researchers'. The importance of research literacy for the profession cannot be ignored. This competence is crucial in enabling practitioners to critically analyse their classroom practice, the classroom-based research they undertake and the research evidence underpinning the education policies they encounter. Given the growing importance and increasing diversity of approaches to evidence synthesis in the world of education (Chong et al., 2024), it is important not only that Early Career Teachers develop an awareness of these forms of research but that they can develop skills in accessing, evaluating and interpreting research evidence using recognised and robust processes. We have witnessed first-hand the potential of this approach to offer opportunities for practitioners to develop evidence-engaged practice through deliberate, sustained and informed critical reflection. In addition, our approach aligns with the standpoints of colleagues writing in this volume, that practitioner researchers will benefit from engaging with a range of research approaches and methods.

Policy documents such as the DE (2016) *Learning Leaders* strategy create a false distinction between the teacher's role as a researcher and as a reflective practitioner. This distinction is deceptive as both positions are profoundly interconnected; they cannot be separated. The capacity of teachers, at all stages of professional learning, to investigate their own practices should not be regarded as separate from their identity as reflective practitioners; instead, both should be intertwined, mutually underpinning the complex vocation that is teaching in the 21st century.

As teacher educators, we too are engaged in ongoing critical reflection on our practice and are committed to continual evaluation of our pedagogical approaches and decision-making through programme and staff review processes. However, the need to address an immediate challenge in our practice required us to be dynamic in an unprecedented way and on a drastically accelerated timescale. This radical rethink created an opportunity for us to respond to the needs of our students and to engage in a more inclusive pedagogy. Over the subsequent cohorts, we retained and developed our 'alternative' assignment and took a collective decision to develop this approach as a core element of our programme. Indeed, we argue that students' awareness and appreciation of the value and contribution of research evidence to their own critical reflective practice has been enhanced by engaging in this assessment.

Our approach to assessing students in this way equips them to navigate the complexities and nuances of adopting evidence-based approaches in their practice. Not only do we seek to enable future practitioners to consider and evaluate the extent to which their professional practice supports the evolving needs of their learners; our hope is that they are equally well-equipped to apply research-engaged and -informed approaches to their critical reflections on broader educational issues.

References

Carr, W., & Kemmis, S. (1986). *Becoming critical: Education, knowledge and action research*. Falmer Press.

Chong, S. W., Bergdahl, N., Bond, M., Miller, S., & Wong, A. W. Y. (2024). Re-imagining 'openness' in *Review of Education*: Methodological standards, open science, and nurturing the next generation of researchers. *Review of Education*, 12(e3468), 1–4. https://doi.org/10.1002/rev3.3468

Coldwell, M., Greany, T., Higgins, S., Brown, C., Maxwell, B., Stiell, B., Stoll, L., Willis, B., & Burns, H. (2017). *Evidence-informed teaching: An evaluation of progress in England (DfE Research report)*. Department for Education. https://assets.publishing.service.gov.uk/government/uploads/system/uploads/attachment_data/file/625007/Evidence-informed_teaching_-_an_evaluation_of_progress_in_England.pdf

Department of Education. (2016). *Learning leaders: A strategy for teacher professional learning*. https://www.education-ni.gov.uk/sites/default/files/publications/de/strategy-document-english.pdf

Dewey, J. (1933). *How we think*. D.C. Heath & Company (Original work published 1910). https://archive.org/details/HowWeThink

Dusty, C. E. (2024). The transformative power of action research. *Educational Action Research*, 32(2), 165–168. https://doi.org/10.1080/09650792.2024.2321728

European Centre for Modern Languages of the Council of Europe. (n.d.). *Professional learning communities.* https://www.ecml.at/ECML-Programme/Programme2016-2019/Professionallearningcommunities/tabid/1868/language/en-GB/Default.aspx

Farrell, T. S. C., & Kennedy, B. (2019). Reflective practice framework for TESOL teachers: One teacher's reflective journey. *Reflective Practice*, 20(1), 1–12. https://doi.org/10.1080/14623943.2018.1539657

Freire, P. (1970). *Pedagogy of the oppressed.* Continuum.

General Teaching Council for Northern Ireland. (GTCNI, 2011). *Teaching: The reflective profession (Incorporating the Northern Ireland teacher competences).* https://www.gtcni.org.uk/assets/files/Resource365/Resources/Publications/The_Reflective_Profession.pdf

Jay, J. K., & Johnson, K. L. (2002). Capturing complexity: A typology of reflective practice for teacher education. *Teaching and Teacher Education*, 18(1), 73–85.

Kemmis, S., McTaggart, R., & Nixon, R. (2014). *The action research planner: Doing critical participatory action research.* Springer. https://www-sciencedirect-com.qub.idm.oclc.org/journal/teaching-and-teacher-education/vol/18/issue/1

Mezirow, J. (1991). *Transformative dimensions of adult learning.* Jossey-Bass.

Pollard, A., Daly, C., Burn, K., & Higgins, S. (2023). *Reflective teaching in secondary schools.* Bloomsbury Publishing.

Sachs, J. (2001). Teacher professional identity: Competing discourses, competing outcomes. *Journal of Education Policy*, 16(2), 149–161. https://doi.org/10.1080/02680930116819

Saunders, L. (2017). Just what is 'evidence-based' teaching? Or 'research-informed' teaching? Or 'inquiry-led' teaching? *IOE Blog.* https://blogs.ucl.ac.uk/ioe/2017/03/23/just-what-is-evidence-based-teaching-or-research-informed-teaching-or-inquiry-led-teaching/

Schön, D. A. (1987). *Educating the reflective practitioner.* Jossey-Bass.

Stenhouse, L. (1985). *Research as a basis for teaching: Readings from the work of Lawrence Stenhouse* (J. Rudduck & D. Hopkins, Eds.). Heinemann Educational Books.

Introduction to Section 4: Research Knowledge, Quality, and Ethics in Practitioner Research

Kate Mawson
Nottingham Trent University, UK

As education increasingly recognises the importance of integrating research into everyday practice, practitioner researchers find themselves navigating a complex and often challenging landscape. Balancing research rigour with practical relevance, upholding ethical standards, and negotiating issues of positionality are all crucial to ensuring that research drives meaningful, inclusive, and transformative change within educational settings.

Across this section, contributors explore how practitioner research can be both methodologically robust and socially responsible. Newby, Lee, and Lee foreground the importance of critical theory as a framework for enhancing the quality and impact of research partnerships. They advocate for an approach that is reflexive, participatory, and attentive to power dynamics, arguing that practitioner research should move beyond traditional positivist models towards knowledge creation that is genuinely inclusive and transformative. This critical stance is essential in ensuring that research addresses the real-world needs of practitioners, learners, and communities rather than reproducing existing hierarchies.

The ethical dimensions of practitioner research are a central thread running through the chapters. Twiner and colleagues remind us that ethics cannot be treated as a procedural checklist;

instead, ethical practice must be woven into every stage of the research process. Reflecting on dilemmas such as confidentiality, informed consent, and the relational complexities of insider research, they urge practitioner researchers to remain critically alert to the responsibilities they hold when researching within their own environments. These concerns are echoed in John Parkin's contribution, which delves deeper into the intricacies of insider-outsider dynamics. Parkin examines how dual roles can create tensions and power imbalances that affect trust, confidentiality, and the interpretation of findings, offering strategies for maintaining ethical integrity while navigating these blurred boundaries.

A complementary strand of the section considers how research can be embedded into teaching practice itself. The chapter on Exploratory Practice exemplifies an iterative model of inquiry, where reflection and action are intertwined in a continuous cycle of professional learning. This approach positions research not as an external imposition but as an integral part of responsive, student-centred pedagogy.

Bringing these ideas together, Formby's chapter on Dialogical Knowledge Curation illustrates how research can become a genuinely collaborative enterprise. By emphasising the importance of mutual respect and shared leadership between practitioners and researchers, Formby shows how research can simultaneously preserve practitioner agency and generate contextually grounded, practically applicable knowledge.

Together, these contributions present practitioner research as a deeply relational and ethical endeavour. Rather than a straightforward application of methods, practitioner research is shown to be a dynamic, critically engaged, and ethically grounded practice – one that has the potential to empower educators, foster authentic partnerships, and contribute to more equitable and inclusive educational environments.

CHAPTER 15

How the Quality of Research and Research Partnerships (Practitioner Researcher) Can Be Enhanced by Using Critical Theory as a Framework

Kate Newby, Matthew Lee and Amanda Lee
University of Sunderland, UK

ABSTRACT

This chapter discusses how critical theory can enhance the quality of practitioner research and research partnerships by addressing power dynamics and promoting participatory, collaborative approaches. Rooted in the works of Marx, Freire, and others, critical theory emphasises the subjective nature of knowledge and the role of power in shaping social structures. By integrating critical theory, practitioner researchers can foster more authentic relationships with communities, ensure ethical research practices, and produce socially transformative outcomes. This framework encourages reflexivity and the active inclusion of marginalised voices throughout the research process.

Keywords: Critical theory; participatory research; power dynamics; practitioner research; reflexivity; research partnerships

Introduction

The basis of true participatory research is the development of authentic relationships between the research team and the community which we are researching to enhance research outcomes. This relationship is mutually beneficial as by having an insider's understanding of the social interactions, we can more accurately interpret the information gathered and interactions observed with less risk of interpreting through our own positional lens. Similarly, as active participants in the research design, conduct and analysis, the research partners can help to provide perspective, but also guide us towards avenues of research or phenomena which may have otherwise gone overlooked. Critical theory, rooted in the works of Karl Marx, Paolo Freire, Max Horkheimer, and Theodor Adorno, emerged as a response to the limitations of traditional positivist approaches to social science research. While positivism prioritises objective observation and quantifiable data (Crotty, 1998), critical theory acknowledges the subjective nature of human experience and the role of power dynamics in shaping social structures and processes (Guba & Lincoln, 1985). Central to critical theory is the recognition that knowledge production is intrinsically political and influenced by the interests and values of dominant groups within society.

Discussion

Critical Theory

Building effective collaborative partnerships between practitioners and academic researchers can enhance the quality and impact of practitioner research. These partnerships or communities of practice should be based on mutual respect, shared goals, and equitable collaboration. Wenger (1998) discusses the concept of communities of practice, where collaboration leads to shared learning and improved practices. Critical theory provides a robust framework for enhancing the quality of research and research partnerships by promoting reflexivity, emancipation, and a critical examination of power structures. Researchers such as Habermas (1984) and Horkheimer (1972) laid foundational perspectives that continue to influence contemporary critical research methodologies. By integrating critical theory, we can produce high-quality, ethical, and impactful practitioner research. As practitioner researchers, we should consider the world around us and in which we undertake research. This leads us to reflect on what is known and unknown and how we create this knowledge and understanding. Considering any potential or actual barriers to this, means considering systemic barriers and the roles they play in knowledge acquisition. To this extent, applying critical theory means considering just this and what we need to do to make our research more meaningful.

Applying Critical Theory as a Framework

Foucault (1980) explores how power operates within social systems, including research settings. By examining who controls the research agenda, whose voices are heard, and who benefits from the research, critical theory promotes more equitable and inclusive research practices. This can lead to more authentic and meaningful partnerships, especially with marginalised or underrepresented groups.

Using critical theory as the framework for the formation of these research partnerships is powerful, as critical theory recognises the intrinsic power dynamics at play in society. Basing partnership relationships on this foundational belief that there are systems of power and control that disproportionately affect marginalised groups, will lead to the development of trust between the researchers and their partners. For example, in a study conducted by Witenstein and Niese (2019), critical theory was used in participatory research and applied to better understand the educational barriers faced by immigrant students in a community college. By recognising the systemic power dynamics, the researchers were able to develop more effective strategies to support these students and offer steps to move forward with institutional and individual recommendations aiming to achieve higher engagement and success rates.

Recognising that we are indeed novices, dependent on the situations we immerse ourselves within, can itself be challenging but by embracing critical theory we can do just this. Appreciating the value and input which the individuals and the communities we are researching have within the research we are conducting means engagement at each of the stages from design to dissemination and each stage in between. Moving beyond the potentially 'tokenistic' approaches means to meaningfully embrace that we ourselves do not know everyone and nor should we especially when we are seeking new knowledge. However, this holds the caveat that we are open to new information which may contradict our own beliefs and personal values.

Quality of Research

Addressing Power Imbalances

As practitioner researchers, we are situated within the field of research, and therefore susceptible to external influences and the mechanisms of power and control that will also be experienced by the research participants. By using participatory research, we aim to redress power imbalances and 'level the playing field' for those who are being researched.

By considering theoretical underpinnings such as critical theory, we can consider both historic and current events and how they may influence participant-researcher relationships as well as the engagement levels and outcomes of the research. For example, travelling communities are a group which have been historically and presently marginalised, ostracised, and stigmatised which means that they may be cautious of engagement with researchers outside of their community and suspicious of their interpretations, for instance, will researchers use a deficit model approach (Condon et al., 2019)? Building up relationships with the community prior to research beginning and developing a partnership approach to the research will allow for a more nuanced interpretation of social phenomena and a more critical interpretation of the results.

Nkoane (2010) identifies that higher education institutions must develop a critical consciousness that addresses the marginalisation of certain groups within academia, in this case focusing on students with special educational needs. Nkoane (2010) poses that traditional academic systems perpetuate inequalities and exclude the voices of marginalised communities, and advocates for a transformative approach to education that prioritises inclusion and empowerment of marginalised voices.

Participatory Practitioner Research

Involving Students in Research

To this extent, participatory practitioner research can be an excellent method to actively involve our students at all stages in pedagogical research, directly benefiting them and reflecting their experiences and time at university. It can be empowering and emancipating (or potentially marginalising), meaning consideration must be given to the potential issues of power imbalances when involving our own students within personal research projects. For example, are students partners in collaboration with equal voice or is their involvement merely performative allyship in a tokenistic demonstration of inclusivity/participation agenda? The value or truth of the inquiry is perhaps dependent on how the data is received and acted on by practitioners (Alvesson, 2002) so the weight that the students' voice, as collaborators, carries is essential to the outcomes.

The disengagement which can occur at times within research education can be mitigated through a research approach which can be seen as more meaningful and inclusive. In a world where people look to see themselves in both education and research, having an approach which addresses this can be especially important.

Researcher Positionality and Bias

The next stage is to support researchers whether, student, novice or experienced researchers to understand their own positionality and bias. The insider-outsider debate being particularly relevant here where we discuss practitioner research (Hammersley, 1993) and explore whether one position compared with the other provides an advantage.

Positionality is typically identified in the context of the three following areas: the subject under investigation, the research participants, and the research context and process (Darwin Holmes, 2020). The process of self-reflection can be a useful tool for researchers to better understand themselves but how many of us do this and if we do engage with reflection is it meaningful?

Probst (2015) explores reflexivity in social work research and states that it is an essential tool that enables us to stay engaged in critical self-awareness throughout the research process. More than simply an ethical tool, reflexivity offers a medium for using self-knowledge to inform and enhance all areas of research.

Sometimes we can be susceptible to external influences such as the people we know, the teams we work in, the organisations we are part of and the locations we live in. A better understanding of this can provide a more effective medium for informing not only ourselves but those who we teach and instruct on research approaches.

Conclusion

Fostering a sound research culture and thereby creating an environment that values and supports research is crucial. This includes sensitivity around the communities involved and sufficient access to resources, time, and training for practitioners involved to effectively engage in research activities. Cochran-Smith and Lytle (2009) emphasise the importance of a supportive research culture in enhancing practitioner inquiry. Heikkinen et al. (2012) discussed the implementation of a peer-group mentorship program where experienced teachers provided guidance and support to novices; this had the impact of significantly enhancing the construction of a professional identity, created more extensive social learning, and variable perspectives.

Agencies such as UK Research and Innovation (UKRI) emphasise the importance of a robust research culture in their strategic objectives to create a world-changing research culture outlined in their UKRI MRC strategic delivery plan (2022–2025). They highlight the need for this in their objectives to focus on the development of world class people and careers, and places. Underpinned by an efficient, effective and agile world class organisation (https://www.ukri.org/publications/mrc-strategic-delivery-plan/).

Using critical theory as a framework for research can enhance the quality and impact of research by promoting reflexivity, addressing power dynamics, and prioritising social justice. By adhering to rigorous criteria for good research and fostering an ambitious approach to practitioner research, we can produce knowledge that is not only academically robust but also ethically sound and socially transformative. Ensuring ethical integrity throughout the research process is crucial to maintaining trust and respect for participants, ultimately leading to more meaningful and impactful research outcomes.

Response to the Editorial Perspective

Whilst there are no overt references, from an editorial perspective, to either the quality of research nor critical theory, there is direct discussion of criticality and partnerships. This could be seen as the direction of discussion with criticality being one of the principal foundations of critical theory. Having the insight and understanding to question what is around someone is crucial to better understanding the world in which we live. This can help to foster relationships with the individuals or communities we research whether we are part of them ourselves or not. Partnerships built from positive relationships can help to advance research not only from the researchers' ideas and notions but those born out of collaboration. Answering questions such as what do people want to know about themselves or others? What is important to them and why? From a critical theory perspective, this also allows us to consider if the research has been created on a positive platform and is it replacing some which has not.

Question for the Reader

How might you apply a critical theoretical framework to your own research or professional practice to help you to uncover and address power imbalances, amplify marginalised voices, and contribute to meaningful social change?

References

Alvesson, M. (2002). *Postmodernism and social research*. Open University Press.

Cochran-Smith, M., & Lytle, S. L. (2009). *Inquiry as stance: Practitioner research for the next generation*. Teachers College Press.

Condon, L., Bedford, H., Ireland, L., Kerr, S., Mytton, J., Richardson, Z., & Jackson, C. (2019). Engaging gypsy, roma, and traveller communities in research: Maximizing opportunities and overcoming challenges. *Qualitative Health Research*, 29(9), 1324–1333. https://doi.org/10.1177/1049732318813

Crotty, M. (1998). *The foundations of social research: Meaning and perspective in the research process*. SAGE Publications Inc.

Foucault, M. (1980). *Power/knowledge: Selected interviews and other writings, 1972-1977*. Pantheon Books.

Guba, E., & Lincoln, Y. (1985). *Naturalistic inquiry*. Sage.

Habermas, J. (1984). *The theory of communicative action: Reason and the rationalization of society* (Vol. 1). Beacon Press.

Hammersley, M. (1993). On the teacher as researcher. *Educational Action Research*, 1(3), 425–445.

Heikkinen, H., Jokinen, H., & Tynjala, P. (2012). *Peer-group mentoring for teacher development*. Routledge.

Holmes, A. G. D. (2020). Researcher positionality – A consideration of its influence and place in qualitative research – A new researcher guide. *International Journal of Education*, 8(4), 1–10.

Horkheimer, M. (1972). *Critical theory: Selected essays*. Continuum International Publishing Group.

Nkoane, M. M. (2010). Listening to voices of the voiceless: A critical consciousness for academic industrial complex. *South African Journal of Higher Education*, 24(3), 317–341.

Probst, B. (2015). The eye regards itself: Benefits and challenges of reflexivity in qualitative social work research. *Social Work Research*, 39(1), 31–40.

Wenger, E. (1998). *Communities of practice: Learning, meaning, and identity*. Cambridge University Press.

Witenstein, M. A., & Niese, M. (2019). Applying guiding principles to resist erasure of immigrant community college students in an ever-changing climate through a critical theory of love. *Journal of Applied Research in the Community College, 26*(2), 1–10.

CHAPTER 16

Unpacking and Underpinning the Ethical Conduct and Sharing of Practitioner Research

Alison Twiner, Patrick Carmichael, Pete Dudley, Sara Hennessy and Ying Ji
Hughes Hall, University of Cambridge, UK

ABSTRACT

Ethics are important in all research, but there are additional considerations when conducting and sharing research into our own contexts of practice. The chapter unpack some barriers and explores mechanisms and practices that can support conducting and sharing ethical practitioner research. The authors argue this represents a wider ethical responsibility: to maximise, diversify and share learning and benefits from research, whilst centrally embedding reflexive, ethical care for participants at the heart of researching our own practice.

Keywords: Practitioner inquiry; research ethics; ethical care; ethical responsibility; publication; sharing professional learning; reflexivity

Introduction

Identifying and considering potential ethical issues is fundamental to research. In universities and other research organisations, there are usually committees, procedures, forms, and monitoring mechanisms that review and approve ethical applications, before research commences. There are also organisations such as BERA – the British Educational Research Association, a key reference point within research conducted in Britain – to which researchers refer in considering ethical issues (BERA, 2024). Within practitioner research, such mechanisms, procedural and social infrastructures are often less formally established, invisible, or entirely absent – potentially leaving practitioners feeling isolated or without a community of practitioner-researchers on which to call and in which to belong. This does not, of course, mean practitioner research is uninformed about ethical research and practice. Indeed, it is the tacit, embedded ethical practice as an underpinning for ethical research (Fox et al., 2007) which we encourage practitioners to celebrate, reflexively unpack and make transparent – on which we elaborate in this chapter – in supporting and publishing practitioner research through Camtree: The Cambridge Teacher Research Exchange. (Camtree – https://camtree.org – is a global platform established to support, promote and publish practitioner research. Through this, we seek to shift the balance and amplify the voice and expertise of practitioner research, as an authentic body of evidence impacting practice, research and policy.) Through such mechanisms and profile raising, reflective and reflexive practitioner research at scale can be considered a collaborative, agentic, rigorous and ethical endeavour – which should and can be shared for wider benefit.

Discussion

Key Arguments and Approaches

Stenhouse (1975) advocated for a 'research stance' to teaching: where practitioners are curious about, and have agency to explore, how to improve their teaching to benefit learners. Cochran-Smith and Lytle (2007) also refer to 'inquiry as stance' within practice: a mindset towards continually reflecting on teaching practice. Where practitioners explore issues of practice through inquiry, or conduct inquiries in Continuing Professional Development (CPD), there is an implicit ethical practice within their professional ideology (Eraut, 2004), alongside more general but crucial aspects, including safeguarding and data protection. However, conducting an inquiry with the intention of sharing it – through publication – raises additional ethical questions. It is the scaffolding around these additional questions we are seeking to embed through Camtree, through courses and transparent peer-review criteria for publication, whereby ethically-sound practitioner research can be recognised as a legitimate and trusted voice in the global knowledge base (or practice base, as called for by Biesta, 2024) and policy-making around educational practice.

Unpacking how to support ethical conduct and sharing of practitioner research, we start by addressing a simple but common dilemma:

It is usually easier, ethically, NOT to share findings of practitioner research.

This is perhaps true, but the same could be said for all research. But it runs counter to the ethics involved in sharing learning from research for wider benefit – a responsibility for educational researchers (BERA, 2024). When considering the value of local expertise and understanding in practitioner research – if all practitioners felt this, there could be little community or collaborative practice.

We can turn this issue on its head, to propose:

In the interests of ethical research community building, we must reduce barriers to sharing practitioner research where insights gained could have wider benefit, and reduce inequity in the knowledge base of education practice.

Camtree is working to act on this position statement. In this, we refer back to the professional ideology of practice, and mechanisms in many education contexts that support good practice, which could be foundations towards ethical research practice. Examples include

- risk assessment and safeguarding processes;
- having a dialogic ethos with learners – to explain why something is being tried, and how it will hopefully benefit learners;
- open communications with colleagues (Stenhouse, 1975) and other stakeholders, including parents;
- and sharing challenges and successes, feeding into a wider cycle of professional learning, as beneficial for professional wellbeing and development (with Groundwater-Smith and Mockler calling for the value of sharing practitioner research 'beyond celebration', 2005).

Drawing on these and similar mechanisms, there are important questions to consider in working towards ethical conduct and sharing of practitioner research, before addressing wider benchmarks such as BERA's guidelines.

Firstly, an issue distinct to practitioner research as opposed to academic research:

When does trying to improve practice become research?

Key markers include where something is being explored more deeply than regular practice, particularly where **data** is being gathered with an intent to **share**.

Relatedly, flagged above and again in contrast to most academic research, is the absence of a formal **ethics review committee**. This is when alternative visions of practitioner research as a collaborative initiative are critical, in thinking:

Not who are the gatekeepers of ethical approval, but who (and which spaces) are the enablers of ethical consideration?

Colleagues can be valuable sources of guidance and sounding boards. Informal conversation and regular but brief slots in meetings can support reflective and fundamentally ethical practice and research around it. Reflexive, transparent reporting on collaborative processes arguably offers more insight as to practitioners' ethical approach than a statement that initial institutional ethical approval was gained, or that research adhered to BERA's guidelines.

At this point, we draw on some of BERA's 'responsibilities to participants', in the 2024 5th edition guidelines, and contextualise considerations within a practitioner-research frame. The responsibilities are

- Consent
- Transparency
- Right to withdraw
- Incentives
- Harm arising from participation in research
- Privacy and data storage
- Disclosure.

There is not enough space to address all seven here, but some can be usefully grouped for consideration. For instance, as illustrated in BERA's guidance:

> *It is normally expected that participants'* **voluntary informed consent** *to be involved in a study will be obtained at the start of the study, and that researchers will remain sensitive and open to the* **possibility that participants may wish,** *for any reason and at any time, to* **withdraw their consent.** *(emphasis added, p. 13)*

That consent should be 'voluntary', amendable and 'informed' necessitates transparency, thus linking the first three responsibilities. Furthermore, referring specifically to practitioner research, there is a need for transparency between what is practice and what is researched practice – whereby participants/learners need to know what they are expected to participate in (practice), and what they can refuse or withdraw from (research about practice).

We can consider **privacy, harm and disclosure** aligned to anonymity and confidentiality, aiming to prevent possible re-identification of involved people other than the author. Using pseudonyms or fictionalising is one option in researchers' responsibilities to participants. Blurring faces or identifiable marks would be critical in photographs or video data – unless express permission has been gained for such data to be shared. Anonymity is however difficult if reporting on research conducted in one's own context, where an author is identifiable to that context. Whilst anonymisation of reported data is the norm, there is recognition – including in BERA's guidelines – that 'anonymity may not always be possible' (p. 22). We then need to ask: can participants **actually** be kept anonymous?

Participants should be supported to understand, in giving informed consent, that whilst they may not be named in reports, if their teacher or colleague is named and locatable to a specific context, re-identification may be possible. This requires more reflection by practitioner researchers as to what data they can present – if any – and how, compared to contexts where anonymity can be guaranteed.

Bringing these elements together, for publication in the Camtree digital library, we have a peer-review process with quality criteria that explicitly require attention to ethical considerations of the research and how they were addressed – whereby points such as the above would be expected to be covered.

Conclusion

At Camtree, we take seriously the responsibility of members of the educational community to communicate findings from research, alongside a need to listen to the experience and expertise of practitioners: which is why the digital library is open access, with all reports freely available. We also take seriously that conducting and publishing ethically rigorous practitioner research brings in additional complications compared to research about practice and contexts outside of our own work. Aligned with Fox et al. (2007), we agree that with support, practitioners themselves are ideally placed to make reflexive, ethical judgements about current and future risk and benefit with regard to participants of inquiries they conduct in their context and into their practice, and to share insights and outcomes from these endeavours. Building on this, through Camtree, we are seeking to build and open up opportunities that support and showcase ethical practitioner research – as a body of knowledge, or practice, and as 'good examples of practice' (Richardson, 2022).

This is also why we support and encourage the sharing of practitioner research reports in any language, and why reports must clearly articulate implications for practice. Relatedly, the ethos of peer review, and training for peer reviewers, is built on the premise of offering feedback aligned to the criteria that supports authors to know what is needed to meet the criteria: as an enabling mechanism towards acceptance for publication, rather than a reason for rejection (for more detail on peer review within Camtree, see https://camtree.org).

Response to the Editorial Perspective

The issues and strategies discussed throughout this chapter resonate with the editorial perspective in balancing procedural and practical elements of ethics. In setting up such an initiative as Camtree, and developing it further, we want to open conversations, share learning, connect and draw people into discussion and communities: with enabling mechanisms rather than barriers, open access to published practitioner research, and low bandwidth requirements of materials as driving principles. Reflexive, ethical and equitable research and practice, in how we operate in building a platform for sharing practitioner research, and to encourage practitioners to use and see this as a valuable place and process, are therefore pivotal to our work. What we also take as critical is how we as a team operate ethically: in supporting practitioners to share research whilst balancing the existing high demands on practitioners' time. This will remain an evolving, reflective process, we hope in conversation and through exchange, publishing and drawing on published practitioner research – with fellow practitioners, researchers and policy makers.

References

Biesta, G. (2024, June). *How much research does teaching need? A case for thoughtfulness* [Keynote presentation]. Close to Practice Research Conference, Nottingham Trent University.

British Educational Research Association [BERA]. (2024). *Ethical guidelines for educational research* (5th ed.). Retrieved August 31, 2024, from www.bera.ac.uk/publication/ethical-guidelines-for-educational-research-2024

Cochran-Smith, M., & Lytle, S. L. (2007). Everything's ethics. Practitioner inquiry and university culture. In A. Campbell & S. Groundwater-Smith (Eds.), *An ethical approach to practitioner research* (pp. 24–41). Routledge Taylor & Francis Group.

Eraut, M. (2004). Transfer of knowledge between education and workplace settings. In H. Rainbird, A. Fuller, & A. Munro (Eds.), *Workplace learning in context* (pp. 201–221). Routledge.

Fox, M., Green, G., & Martin, P. (2007). *Doing practitioner research*. SAGE.

Groundwater-Smith, S., & Mockler, N. (2005, July). *Practitioner research in Education: Beyond Celebration* [Paper presentation]. AARE Focus Conference, James Cook University, Cairns.

Richardson, A. (2022). Introduction: Close-to-Practice research in Holocaust Education. *Holocaust Studies*. https://doi.org/10.1080/17504902.2022.2058724

Stenhouse, L. (1975). *An introduction to curriculum research and development*. Heinemann.

CHAPTER 17

Exploratory Practice: What About the Learners?

Rachel Bate
Idea Store Learning Tower Hamlets, UK

ABSTRACT

Exploratory practice (EP) is organised around a set of guiding principles of which an interest in quality of life is central (Allwright, 2003). Such an emphasis encourages practitioner researchers to broaden their scope beyond 'instructional efficiency' and instead focus on working with others, including learners, to better understand an aspect of classroom-related life which puzzles them.

Keywords: Exploratory Practice; collaborative; dialogue; mutual understanding; sustainable; quality of life

Introduction

Exploratory Practice

At the heart of EP is the integration of language teaching and learning with research in the belief that such an approach has the potential to bring about meaningful and long-lasting developments. Both Hanks (2017) and Allwright (2003) highlight the pursuit of ever greater efficiency, dominant in educational research driven by powerful discourses of improvement and effectiveness. Such research, according to Allwright (2003, p. 104), treats the classroom as an asocial space, looking for simple causal relationships. As EP evolved in the 1990s and early 2000s, Allwright and those he collaborated with sought to counter this through their own practice. Their work led to the evolution of a set of guiding principles to support those who wished to engage in a more sustainable research process. One of the main principles is the promotion of understanding over problem-solving by asking practitioners to reflect upon what puzzles them about life in their classrooms. Learners are also included as practitioners in EP positioning them as necessary and active research participants, instead of objects or subjects of the process. Finally, a concern with quality of life is a further central principle recognising classrooms as social spaces into which teachers and learners bring multiple identities and 'interact with each other in infinitely complex ways' (Hanks, 2017, p. 102).

Discussion

Why EP?

I applied an EP approach to a small-scale research project completed as part of my PhD. I did so as I believed its key principles closely aligned with my motivations for undertaking this research and the overarching dialogic stance I adopted throughout my thesis. In the rest of this section, I therefore review this specific research project and the choices I made in relation to the principles of EP, discussing their implications regarding the quality and ethics of practitioner research in the conclusion.

As someone who began working in English for Speakers of Other Languages (ESOL) in 2005, not long after the launch of the Skills for Life initiative, I have witnessed considerable changes both at a policy level and in mainstream discourses surrounding citizenship and migration. These have had a significant impact on the ESOL classroom with real-life consequences for learners. Baynham (2006, p. 38) discusses the significant role the classroom can play in providing a space for learners to undertake 'an apprenticeship in "speaking out" which may prove of use in other contexts'. After reflecting upon this and my own experience, I became interested in forming a better understanding of the possibilities for learners to develop a voice.[1] I was already aware of the principles of EP before I began my research and credit it with helping to shape my focus and providing a framework to support my investigation. From an EP perspective, concern with quality of life and quality of education are not separate issues but in fact intertwined and seem highly appropriate for the context in which I was working.

Another aspect of my work informed by EP was the prioritising of working for understanding classroom life. As Hanks (2017, p. 91) writes, 'much research in the 20th and 21st centuries is in a tearing hurry to improve before taking the time to understand'. Recognising the ESOL classroom as a complex space serving a variety of functions, I valued the opportunity of undertaking research to analyse what occurred in-depth. In fact, I did not trial anything new, but explored an established pedagogical approach based upon the work of Paulo Freire (see Cooke et al., 2018, regarding this approach). The aim was to gain an insight into evolving classroom dynamics during discussion work and the potential for them to lead to the development of voice. To achieve this, I recorded a discussion and then transcribed and analysed it using two different but complementary approaches. I employed Conversation Analysis to examine the immediate classroom dynamics, and a broader form of analysis related to positionality. As a result, I was able to draw conclusions about the pedagogical value of the subject matter, including opportunities for a consideration of multilingualism presented for learners to manage the discourse themselves. This was illustrated as learners began to demonstrate their right to impose reception, encouraged by an increase in social and cultural capital due to the subject. Consequently, I reached a deeper understanding of how an existing pedagogical approach could enable learners to develop their individual voices, along with some of the essential contributing factors to this process.

I view the understanding I arrived at above as advancing knowledge regarding the building of individual subjectivities during classroom discussions. This knowledge was gained after a dialogical analysis of the data, recognising that when individuals speak they are always addressing an 'other', which can include a real or imagined audience, consisting of an individual, wider social groups or even specific ideologies (see Pavlenko, 2007; Vitanova, 2013). The concept of dialogue I utilised in my research was taken from the work of Mikhael Bakhtin. From such a perspective, understanding and therefore knowledge are realised through interacting with an 'other'. EP adopts a similar position, also informed by Bakhtin's writing, with Hanks (2017, p. 86) stating, 'our understandings are dependent not only on ourselves, but on interactions with others'. In my own research, my approach to data analysis was dialogic in nature, whilst also seeking out the views and experiences of those who worked and studied in my setting, encouraging both teachers and learners to reflect upon relevant experiences. The increase in my understanding and knowledge over the course of the research emerged out of interactions with others. This I argue, was supported and enhanced by the principles of EP which state that working for understanding should involve everyone and be a collaborative act.

In the final paragraph, where I consider my own research, I would like to highlight one of its possible limitations when compared to the guidelines of EP. Along with the key principles of quality of life and working for understanding, a persistent theme in EP is working collaboratively for mutual development. Although, as discussed above, I did work with both teachers and learners, the focus, research design, analysis and writing of findings were all directed by myself. There was clearly more I could have done to increase opportunities for collaborative working. It is an issue I return to in my concluding thoughts below in relation to the quality and ethics of research.

Conclusion

The president of BERA introduces the updated Ethical Guidelines for Educational Research by reminding researchers not only of their responsibilities to protect participants but also to 'promote their rights to participation' (Baumfield, 2024, p. 6), and it is this particular aspect of ethics I consider here. The principles of EP promote the inclusion of learners as co-researchers whose contributions are viewed as necessary when working for an understanding of classroom life. Learners like teachers are seen as practitioners in the classroom with valuable knowledge, insights and experiences. In BERA's statement regarding Close-to-Practice (CtP) educational research, it is recommended that the voices of practitioners are included at all stages of the research process to increase the chances of success (BERA, 2018, p. 3). From an EP perspective, this would mean the inclusion of learner voices, a possibility promoted by others in the field of educational research (see, for example, Ball, 2013; Fielding, 2004). There is an added ethical dimension to this as when learners become researchers in their own right opportunities to develop highly valued research-based skills can open up for them (for an example of this, see Cooke et al., 2018). Through the inclusion of learners as co-researchers, we would begin to answer Biesta's call for the democratisation of knowledge, recognising the possibility for all in education to participate in its advancement (Biesta, 2020, p. 146).

Response to the Editorial Perspective

In EP, understanding and knowledge are gained by interacting with others in specific contexts. This I believe is not too dissimilar from Biesta's (2020) discussion of Dewey's pragmatism which looks beyond both objectivism and relativism to view knowledge as being constructed in a transactional process. All actors in the classroom are encouraged to collaborate in the generation of knowledge, challenging traditional hierarchical structures. As a practitioner researcher, who is often the main class teacher, attempting to do so is not without challenges. However, I have found reflecting upon the principles of EP, especially the aim to improve quality of life, to be a useful tool in this process as it has the potential to bring learners' voices to the fore.

Allwright (2013) contrasts practitioner research with educational research into effectiveness, which he labels as 'theorizing up' as complex problems based in the real world become simplified to allow for generalisation. Practitioner research on the other hand with specific reference to EP, Allwright (2013) argues, is 'theorizing down' looking deeper into this complexity. In this instance, discussions of quality are framed around how research supports practitioners in gaining deeper insights into their practice, meeting locally determined needs. These can be built upon an academically rigorous process with clear research questions, a methodology and the selection of appropriate methods, but grounded in a dialogue which values heterogeneity, as discussed in the Editorial Perspective.

Finally, when practitioners, including learners, research their own settings they collaborate to develop not only context-specific knowledge, but also potentially new ways of working together. Allwright (2013) argues this is how EP, and practitioner research in general, can contribute to bringing about change in education. The value of practitioner research and its pragmatic outlook is the neverending potential for it to evolve to support those inhabiting the field of education to better understand the contexts they work in along with the advancement of knowledge.

Question for the Reader

Can you think of an aspect of classroom life you would like to better understand?

Note

1. I define the term voice drawing upon the work of Bakhtin (1981), who employs it to denote an individual's intentional use of language to express a perspective of the world.

References

Allwright, D. (2003). Exploratory practice: Rethinking practitioner research in language teaching research. *Language Teaching Research*, 7(2), 113–141.

Allwright, D. (2013). Theorizing "down" instead of "up": The special contribution of exploratory practice. *KOTESOL Proceedings*, pp. 11–28.

Bakhtin, M. M. (1981). *The dialogic imagination: four essays*. [Edited by Holquist, H. Translated by Emerson, C. and Holquist, H]. University of Texas Press.

Ball, S. J. (2013). *Education, justice and democracy: The struggle over ignorance and opportunity*. Centre for Labour and Social Studies.

Baumfield, V. (2024). Letter from the President. (2024) *Ethical Guidelines for Educational Research* (5th ed.). British Educational Research Association [BERA]. Retrieved August 21, 2024, from https://www.bera.ac.uk/publication/ethical-guidelines-for-educational-research-2024

Baynham, M. (2006). Agency and contingency in the language learning of refugees and asylum seekers. *Linguistics and Education*, 17, 24–39.

Biesta, G. (2020). *Educational research: An unorthodox introduction*. Bloomsbury Academic.

British Educational Research Association [BERA]. (2018). *Close to practice research: A BERA statement*. Retrieved August 21, 2024, from https://www.bera.ac.uk/publication/bera-statement-on-close-to-practice-research

Cooke, M., Bryers, D., & Winstanley, B. (2018). 'Our languages': Towards sociolinguistic citizenship in ESOL. *Working Papers in Urban Language & Literacies*, Paper 234. Retrieved September 12, 2018, fromhttps://www.academia.edu/35839204/WP234_Cooke_Bryers_and_Winstanley_2018_Our_Languages_Sociolinguistics_in_multilingual_participatory_ESOL_classes

Fielding, M. (2004). "New wave" student voice and the renewal of civic society. *London Review of Education*, 2(3), 197–217.

Hanks, J. (2017). *Exploratory practice in language learning: Puzzling principles and practices*. Palgrave Macmillan.

Pavlenko, A. (2007). Autobiographic narratives as data in applied linguistics. *Applied Linguistics*, 28(2), 163–188.

Vitanova, G. (2013). Narratives as zones of dialogical constructions: A Bakhtinian approach to data in qualitative research. *Critical inquiries in Language Studies*, 10(3), 242–261.

CHAPTER 18

Managing Ethical Dilemmas with the Dual Identity of Practitioner and Researcher

John Parkin
Anglia Ruskin University, UK

ABSTRACT

This chapter presents research by a male Senior Lecturer Practitioner in Education and doctoral researcher who had also previously worked as a primary school teacher. The research explores the experiences of male undergraduate students completing a BA Primary Education Studies degree in an English university. The chapter examines the ethical challenges encountered by a practitioner-researcher navigating the dual roles of university lecturer and doctoral researcher. Key themes include power dynamics, confidentiality and the complexities of occupying an insider -outsider position as a researcher.

Keywords: Insider/outsider; researcher-practitioner; ethics; masculinities; male primary school teacher; confidentiality; trust; power imbalance

Introduction

This chapter explores how I navigated ethical dilemmas as an insider/outsider researcher-practitioner when teaching and undertaking research with undergraduates I was teaching.

Knowledge is situated and understood through relationships, which leads to the significance of the researcher's position related to the study (Bukamal, 2022). As a cisgender male former primary school teacher, I shared commonalities with male students participating in my study exploring the experiences of males completing an undergraduate PES degree. In line with Dwyer and Buckle (2009), my position as researcher showed fluid traits of outsider and insider. To a degree I was an insider as a male who had taught younger children as a career which led to further commonalities with some of the males in the study (Coghlan & Brydon-Miller, 2014). I also showed elements of being an insider with my professional role of senior lecturer practitioner teaching some students in the study, which led to my acceptance as a researcher by students who knew me (Dwyer & Buckle, 2009). However, I also showed elements of an outsider researcher 'standing at a distance' (Chhabra, 2020, p. 307) from the participating students as a man who was known to the students teaching on the course and a former primary school teacher: roles and experiences participating students did not yet have.

I was an 'in-betweener' (Chhabra, 2020, p. 308) inhabiting a space between insider and outsider. In this liminal space, I was simultaneously an insider and an outsider (Bukamal, 2022). For instance, I was an insider with men completing the PES degree in terms of understanding the complexities of men working with young children, but I was an outsider to participants who were beginning their careers in education while I had 17 years of experience as a man teaching in primary schools.

Discussion

Navigating Researcher Positionality and Ethical Dilemmas

At the time of the study, between 2020 and 2023, I was working as a Senior Lecturer Practitioner in Education in a large post-1992 university recruiting students from a diverse range of backgrounds. I was teaching modules part of an undergraduate PES programme which developed the content knowledge and pedagogical content knowledge (Shulman & Shulman, 2004) of the National Curriculum for 5-to-11-year-old children in

England. I observed male undergraduates completing the course were a small proportion of students and more likely to encounter challenges with continuing with the degree. My study consisted of two stages. Firstly, I wanted to understand why these male students joined a numerically female dominated degree course and their experiences both inside and outside the course. Secondly, I delivered workshops for PES students of all genders exploring gender in the classroom which were evaluated using focus group interviews. Ethical considerations as a researcher-practitioner permeated all my study.

A power imbalance often exists between researcher and participant (Råheim et al., 2016). Lecturers hold more perceived or actual power than students in what Ferguson et al. (2004, p. 57) describe as a 'fiduciary relationship' in which students place trust and reliance on the lecturer in their role. Teaching some of the participants presented the risk that students could feel a perceived obligation to participate due to my power as a lecturer. I tried to minimise this power imbalance by emphasising to participants that students were not obliged to participate, and that I had two separate roles as researcher and lecturer. When recruiting potential participants, I asked course leaders of PES programmes on different campuses of the university to share my participant recruitment announcements as I felt if I did so more perceived pressure could be applied to students to participate.

However, reducing this power imbalance in the study had implications for my teaching relationship with students if the balance changed significantly. For instance, my interpretation of a situation was one participant stated to the rest of the class they would see me later during the day to participate in a workshop to emphasise to other students they were taking part. Power is a fluid force which can often be hidden (Czerniawski, 2023), which I realised by teaching and assessing students who I was relying on to participate in my study. Teaching and researching with the same students could be a source of bias as I could base my analysis on my previous perceptions of students from lectures and analyse the research setting on my previous professional and teaching experiences. I also acknowledged that roles and relationships with participants in the past, present and future would influence by research (Holian & Coghlan, 2013).

Trust and respect are essential factors in the relationship between researcher and participant (British Educational Research Association, 2024). These factors are also vital in the relationship between lecturer and student. Nikkanen (2019) explains that as a teacher-researcher she felt her role as a teacher informed her ethical behaviour more than that of being a researcher due to the ongoing professional relationship with students and the expectation of having a positive impact on them. Similarly, I felt a greater ethical responsibility to participating students as a lecturer than a researcher. For instance, I aimed to arrange interviews and workshops outside of assessment periods so students could focus on academic work.

Confidentiality as a practitioner-researcher was an important consideration. In my dual role as lecturer and researcher, I made my researcher role explicit and clear to participating students in research activities to minimise any tensions over my role as lecturer and researcher (British Educational Research Association, 2024). In line with Mercer (2007), I was mindful of emphasising to participants in ethics paperwork and before interviews that I would keep information confidential, but I was also mindful about how I shared information within the university where I worked. As a practitioner-researcher, I continued to work and be present in the research setting (Poulton, 2023), teaching undergraduates who participated in my study. This factor is different to many other researchers who complete research in a specific location or community and then depart. In one instance, I told students in a seminar that I was going to present a research poster at a conference the next day. The students wanted to see the poster, but a male student who had participated in the set of initial semi-structured interviews was in the seminar. Consequently, I had to recollect if I had used any quotations from his interview before showing the poster to the students in case he was identifiable or felt uncomfortable his words were being shared with peers. I had not used any quotations from him, so I was able to share the poster in the session. This example illustrates that a practitioner-researcher needs to protect confidentiality after the completion of research as researcher and participants may still be working or studying in the same setting (Poulton, 2023). This scenario shows the ongoing ethical dilemmas existing in the dual role of practitioner and lecturer.

Conclusion

This interaction of professional and personal identities led to the simplistic binary of insider/outsider being inapplicable to my position as a researcher (Dwyer & Buckle, 2009). This interaction applies to my dual role of practitioner-researcher. The Editorial emphasises the role of power in practitioner research. In my case study, I have discussed how the position of power I held as a Senior Lecturer Practitioner in relation to undergraduates I taught was a factor in my ethical considerations. Furthermore, power was a dynamic force which ebbed, flowed and changed across and beyond my study. My ethics application to the university research panel helped my consider ethical processes, but throughout and beyond my study I considered ethics-in-practice and how my dual work as practitioner and researcher influenced by actions and behaviour.

Response to the Editorial Perspective

I acknowledge that being a practitioner-researcher presented ethical challenges in terms of power and responsibilities, but my dual insider/outsider role gave me insights into the study which would have been possible if I held a different position in relation to my research. By working 'close-to-practice' I learnt about the experiences, opportunities and barriers faced by males completing the PES degree which influenced my practice and that of colleagues. Although not discussed in this chapter, investigating my context led to enhancements in understanding and supporting males completing an undergraduate PES degree.

Questions for the Reader

1. What are the ethical dilemmas of being both a practitioner and researcher in your own research? How can you manage these risks?

2. How can you minimise the power imbalance between yourself and your participants?

References

British Education Research Association. (2024). *Ethical guidelines for educational research* (4th ed.). British Educational Research Association.

Bukamal, H. (2022). Deconstructing insider–outsider researcher positionality. *British Journal of Special Education*, 49(3), 327–349. https://doi.org/10.1111/1467-8578.12426

Chhabra, G. (2020). Insider, outsider or an in-betweener? Epistemological reflections of a legally blind researcher on conducting cross-national disability research. 22(1), Article 1. https://doi.org/10.16993/sjdr.696

Coghlan, D., & Brydon-Miller, M. (2014). *The SAGE encyclopedia of action research*. SAGE Publications Ltd. https://doi.org/10.4135/9781446294406

Czerniawski, G. (2023). Power, positionality and practitioner research: Schoolteachers' experiences of professional doctorates in education. *British Educational Research Journal*, 49(6), 1372–1386. https://doi.org/10.1002/berj.3902

Dwyer, S. C., & Buckle, J. L. (2009). The space between: On being an insider-outsider in qualitative research. *International Journal of Qualitative Methods*, 8(1), 54–63. https://doi.org/10.1177/160940690900800105

Ferguson, L. M., Yonge, O., & Myrick, F. (2004). Students' involvement in faculty research: Ethical and methodological issues. *International Journal of Qualitative Methods*, 3(4), 56–68. https://doi.org/10.1177/160940690400300405

Holian, R., & Coghlan, D. (2013). Ethical issues and role duality in insider action research: Challenges for action research degree programmes. *Systemic Practice and Action Research*, 26(5), 399–415. https://doi.org/10.1007/s11213-012-9256-6

Mercer, J. (2007). The challenges of insider research in educational institutions: Wielding a double-edged sword and resolving delicate dilemmas. *Oxford Review of Education*, 33(1), 1–17. https://doi.org/10.1080/03054980601094651

Nikkanen, H. M. (2019). Double agent?: Ethical considerations in conducting ethnography as a teacher-researcher. In *Implementing ethics in educational ethnography*. Routledge.

Poulton, P. (2023). Being a teacher-researcher: Reflections on an insider research project from a virtues-based approach to research ethics. *Educational Action Research, 31*(3), 575–591. https://doi.org/10.1080/09650792.2021.1962379

Råheim, M., Magnussen, L. H., Sekse, R. J. T., Lunde, Å., Jacobsen, T., & Blystad, A. (2016). Researcher–researched relationship in qualitative research: Shifts in positions and researcher vulnerability. *International Journal of Qualitative Studies on Health and Well-Being, 11*(1), 30996. https://doi.org/10.3402/qhw.v11.30996

Shulman, L. S., & Shulman, J. H. (2004). How and what teachers learn: A shifting perspective. *Journal of Curriculum Studies, 36*(2), 257–271. https://doi.org/10.1080/0022027032000148298

CHAPTER 19

Dialogical Knowledge Curation in Education: Integrating Research and Practice in North East Wales

Tomos G. ap Sion, Lisa Formby, Sue Horder and Karen Rhys Jones
Wrexham University, UK

ABSTRACT

This chapter explores the concept of Dialogical Knowledge Curation, an approach that brings practitioners and researchers together to increase the efficacy of research in educational practice. A form of 'knowledge brokering', Dialogical Knowledge Curation has two key components. The first, 'dialogical', component embodies the collaborative and interactive aspects of knowledge brokering, emphasising the importance of discussion, collaboration, and relationship building. The second, 'knowledge curation', component accentuates an often-overlooked method of knowledge brokering, where researchers – or other parties – assemble numerous related ideas on a particular topic for practitioners to explore as a collection. Through these two components, it is our hope that Dialogical Knowledge Curation may offer an approach which helps ensure that transformed research is accessible and relevant for practitioners, while also preserving their agency. This represents an innovative approach where researchers do 'what they do best' by building and supporting a research foundation for practitioners, and practitioners do what they do best by embedding this foundation within their context. Through open discussion and meaningful relationships, both perspectives are united – resulting in an empowering learning culture.

Keywords: Knowledge brokering; knowledge mobilisation; research-informed practice; inquiry-based teaching; teacher agency; school-university partnerships; partnership working; teacher development

Introduction

In a landscape that increasingly values the notion of being 'evidence-informed', practitioners are finding that more is being asked of them. This especially holds in Wales, where practitioners are not only adapting to a recently introduced and pioneering Curriculum (Welsh Government, 2023), but are also encouraged to use and contribute to educational research (Welsh Government, 2021). While laudable in its ambition, practitioners require – perhaps now more than ever – the support to make this national vision a reality. In this chapter, we will explore a concept we have called Dialogical Knowledge Curation, a form of knowledge brokering aiming to bridge the gap between research and practice. We will explore this concept through a case study involving a school we worked with, concluding that Dialogical Knowledge Curation could make research more accessible, relevant, and realistic for practitioners to use, while also preserving their agency. Through this exploration, it is our hope to spark the imagination of researchers and practitioners alike, helping to bring both parties together in order to make the goal of an evidence-informed education profession a reality.

Discussion

Increasing the prominence of research within the education ecosystem has long been thought to be beneficial (Slavin, 2004), with numerous 'evidence-informed' programmes developed to increase the quality and comprehensibility of research and its impact on practice (Higgins et al., 2022; James & Pollard, 2011; Nelson & Campbell, 2017). Relatedly, utilising research within education is also becoming a priority for many governments (Sjölund et al., 2022). For instance, it is the aim of the Welsh Government that all educational policy and practice be underpinned by robust and rigorous research as part of its drive to make the discipline more evidence-informed. This research is to be undertaken by professionals within the education sector – including practitioners (Welsh Government, 2021).

However, effectively integrating research for practitioners to use and contribute to is not straightforward (Higgins, 2018; OECD, 2022), potentially being affected by the quality and accessibility of research, teachers' skillsets and attitudes, school leadership and culture, and also the interactions and support structures within the wider education system (Horder et al., 2025; Rickinson, Sharples, et al., 2020; Rickinson, Walsh, et al., 2020; van Schaik et al., 2018). The traditional 'build it and they will come' model, where research is produced and made available for practitioners, has not been found to be particularly effective, facing issues such as insufficient practitioner time, and the lack of usefulness and accessibility of the research (Rycroft-Smith, 2022). Such issues and complexities suggest a need to identify better ways of integrating research and practice (Rey & Gaussel, 2016).

One proposal towards bridging this gap is 'knowledge brokering' (Chew et al., 2022; Mosher et al., 2014; Rycroft-Smith, 2022). While vaguely defined, the concept can be described as a process whereby research is transformed by 'brokers' to increase research's accessibility, usability, and ultimately its efficacy – supporting its transfer across fields and institutional boundaries. While these brokers can be individuals or groups from a variety of backgrounds, they should have a deep understanding of research and ideally practice, while also being trustworthy and ethical – especially as they can cause harm by misinforming practitioners (Rycroft-smith, 2022).

We have ourselves experienced the difficulties in integrating research and practice within the education system in Wales. Alongside school partners, we developed a novel form of knowledge brokering to address some of these challenges called Dialogical Knowledge Curation. As an initial conceptualisation, the 'dialogical' component can be understood as embodying the collaborative and interactive aspects of knowledge brokering, focusing on providing the space for discussion, collaboration, and relationship building. As noted above, numerous researchers have emphasised the importance of bidirectional and reciprocal relationships (Cornelissen et al., 2015; van Schaik et al., 2018). Dialogical Knowledge Curation strives for the same goal. When researchers and practitioners together co-construct an understanding of what strategies are effective within a context, research may become more relevant, accessible, and ultimately beneficial for practitioners and their learners (Martinovic et al., 2012; van Schaik et al., 2018).

The 'knowledge curation' component of the concept is an overlooked aspect of knowledge brokering, where the broker gathers numerous ideas together on various topics or themes to be explored by practitioners as a collection (Rycroft-Smith, 2022). This could take many forms (e.g. document, presentation, etc.), and each approach would likely have its own strengths and weaknesses. What is important is that brokers *curate* knowledge – whether it be scientific or conceptual – providing practitioners with an informed and justified interpretation of various educational ideas, strategies, or approaches that are, ideally, readily transferable into practice.

We believe that Dialogical Knowledge Curation could mitigate some of the issues facing practitioner research engagement. For instance, emphasising the importance of collaborative dialogue could ensure that research is made accessible for practitioners by enabling them to influence the type and format of the research they receive. Additionally, it might also give brokers the opportunity to support practitioner understanding and interpretation of research.

Dialogical Knowledge Curation could also alleviate some of the practical and skills-related burden associated with research. By shouldering a meaningful portion of the research work, brokers could help protect practitioner time and minimise the research-related training practitioners require to evaluate and interpret research. Furthermore, curating knowledge could be a powerful tool to enhance practitioner agency. Even with strong dialogue, if brokers identify a particular strategy, practitioner choice becomes limited. However, through curating multiple ideas or strategies to explore, practitioner choice is maintained and their agency preserved.

Based on this working understanding of Dialogical Knowledge Curation, we can now introduce some initial findings relating to how university academics could play this brokering role (Horder et al., 2025). In the spring of 2022, we worked with a number of primary schools in North Wales as part of a Welsh Government funded project called Talk Pedagogy, aiming to support schools in their understanding of the pedagogical aspects of the Curriculum in Wales (Welsh Government, 2023).

With one local school in the Wrexham County Borough area, we engaged in a co-constructive process which shares a close alignment with Dialogical Knowledge Curation. Initially, we held three meetings with two to three practitioners from the school. In the first two meetings, we explored in detail the school's context, their aspirations, and how we might be able to support them, aiming to foster an environment of open and honest discussion. Through this reflective process, we arrived at a clearer understanding of the kind of questions the practitioners were interested in, and the learning contexts and lessons in which these questions were to be explored.

Following these two meetings, we created a document that brought together many key research-informed ideas relating to 'collaborative learning' – a pedagogical approach they were interested in. Key aspects of this document include a concise conceptualisation of collaborative learning, an exploration of its efficacy, how it relates to other teaching approaches and the psychology of learning, and, principally, a categorised list of potential directions to explore that can be translated into practice.

Perhaps importantly, the document focused on exploring general principles or ideas that could apply to an array of situations. For example, one category focused on interactions between learners, with sub-categories discussing various ideas on fostering positive interdependence between learners, the role of the practitioner, negotiations within groups, and so on. Multiple options were included throughout, enabling practitioners to explore and reflect on them as an accessible whole and to pursue the ideas in which they saw potential.

Following a number of weeks where the practitioners reflected on and experimented with applying collaborative learning, we met with the practitioners to discuss their progress. The practitioners found the document accessible and 'exactly what I need', making the research easier and less time-consuming to read, understand, and draw on.

> *It was the 'ten pillars' document that we found really useful, partly because it brought lots of other bits of research into one… time-wise, it was quite nice that it was condensed…*

Furthermore, having a document created by researchers they trusted translated into increased confidence in the research. This helped them to explore new and different ideas – even when 'quite unnerving'. This paid dividends, with practitioners noting a number of social, academic, and attitude benefits for learners, including increased confidence, teamworking ability, engagement, and interest.

Practitioners also talked about the document in a manner consistent with the notion of knowledge curation, often emphasising their ability to choose the ideas they saw value in – 'oh I like that, pinch that, pinch that'.

> *We picked out bits we thought would be interesting… so when that [document] focused your attention… yea, it was like real social science…*

While resulting in a number of benefits, the project was largely exploratory, and, in reflection, there were a number of ways we could improve (e.g. the document could have been more accessible). This being said, the collaborative process we engaged in represents a promising approach where both academics and practitioners play to each other's strengths, with open discussions bridging the gap between research and practice. Whilst our research involved university academics playing this brokering role, this could be undertaken by others within their own contexts.

Conclusion

In this chapter, we explored the concept of Dialogical Knowledge Curation, a form of knowledge brokering which we believe could bridge research and practice. By emphasising dialogue and relationship building, Dialogical Knowledge Curation could help ensure that transformed research is accessible and relevant for practitioners, and that researchers are on-hand to support its interpretation. Furthermore, by shouldering a meaningful portion of the research work, researchers could alleviate some of the time and skill-related burden that researching carries. Through curating ideas, practitioner agency could also be enhanced – enabling practitioners to pursue ideas they see as promising.

Response to the Editorial Perspective

The vision set forth by Dialogical Knowledge Curation offers a new way to meet the practitioner researcher role. Instead of individuals occupying a 'third space' between research and practice, this space is bridged through Dialogical Knowledge Curation. Through this truly collaborative and collegial process, both academic and professional fields are united – representing an innovative approach where researchers do 'what they do best' by building and supporting a research foundation, and practitioners do what they do best by embedding this foundation within their context. Through open discussion and meaningful collaboration, both perspectives are integrated – resulting in an empowering learning culture.

Questions for the Reader

When reading this chapter, you may wish to consider the following questions:

1. How could Dialogical Knowledge Curation enhance your practice?

2. How does a layered collaborative approach alleviate concerns facing practitioners engaging with research?

3. How would you go about exploring Dialogical Knowledge Curation? Who would you collaborate with?

References

Chew, S., Armstrong, N., & Martin, G. P. (2022). Understanding knowledge brokerage and its transformative potential: A Bourdieusian perspective. *Evidence and Policy*, *18*(1), 25–42.

Cornelissen, F., Daly, A. J., liou, Y.-H., Van Swet, J., Beijaard, D., & Bergen, T. C. (2015). Leveraging the relationship: Knowledge processes in school–university research networks of master's programmes. *Research Papers in Education*, *30*(3), 366–392.

Higgins, S. (2018). *Improving learning: Meta-analysis of intervention research in education*. Cambridge University Press.

Higgins, S., Katsipataki, M., Villanueva Aguilera, A. B., Dobson, E., Gascoine, L., Rajab, T., Kalambouka, A., Reardon, J., Stafford, J., & Uwimpuhwe, G. (2022). The teaching and learning toolkit: Communicating research evidence to inform decision-making for policy and practice in education. *Review of Education*, *10*, e3327. https://doi.org/10.1002/rev3.3327

Horder, S., ap Sion, T. G., Formby, L., & Rhys Jones, K. (2025). Navigating curriculum uncertainty for teacher agency. In C. Conn, B. Mitchell, & M. Hutt (Eds.), *Working with uncertainty for educational change* (pp. 135–151). Routledge.

James, M., & Pollard, A. (2011). TLRP's ten principles for effective pedagogy: Rationale, development, evidence, argument and impact. *Research Papers in Education*, *26*(3), 275–328.

Martinovic, D., Weib, N., Ratkovic, S., Willard-Holt, C., Spencer, T., & Cantalini-Williams, M. (2012). 'Doing research was inspiring': Building a research community with teachers. *Education Action Research*, *20*(3), 385–406.

Mosher, J., Anucha, U., Appiah, H., & Levesque, S. (2014). From research to action: Four theories and their implications for knowledge mobilisation. *Scholarly and Research Communication*, *5*(3).

Nelson, J., & Campbell, C. (2017). Evidence-informed practice in education: Meanings and applications. *Educational Research*, *59*(2), 127–135.

OECD. (2022). *Who cares about using educational research in policy and practice?: strengthening research engagement, educational research and innovation.* OECD Publishing. https://doi.org/10.1787/d7ff793d-en

Rey, O., & Gaussel, M. (2016). The conditions for the successful use of research results by teachers: Reflections on some innovations in France. *European Journal of Teacher Education, 39*(5), 557–587.

Rickinson, M., Sharples, J., & Lovell, O. (2020). Towards a better understanding of quality of evidence use. In S. Gorard (Ed.), *Getting evidence into education: evaluating the routes to policy and practice* (pp. 3–9). Routledge.

Rickinson, M., Walsh, L., Cirkony, C., Salisbury, M., & Gleeson, J. (2020). *Monash Q project: Quality use of research evidence framework.* Monash University.

Rycroft-Smith, L. (2022). Knowledge brokering to bridge the research-practice gap in education: Where are we now? *Review of Education, 10*, e3341.

Sjölund, S., Lindvall, J., Larsson, M., & Ryve, A. (2022). Using research to inform practice through research-practice partnerships: A systematic literature review. *Review of Education, 10*(1), e3337.

Slavin, R. (2004). Education research can and must address "what works" questions. *Educational Researcher, 33*(1), 27–28.

van Schaik, P., Volman, M., Admiraal, W., & Schencke, W. (2018). Barriers and conditions for teachers' utilisation of academic knowledge. *International Journal of Education Research, 90*, 50–63.

Welsh Government. (2021). *The National Strategy for Educational Research and Enquiry (NSERE): vision document.* The Welsh Government. Retrieved June 16, 2024, from https://www.gov.wales/national-strategy-educational-research-and-enquiry-nsere-vision-document-html

Welsh Government. (2023). *Curriculum for Wales.* Retrieved March 20, 2023, from https://hwb.gov.wales/curriculum-for-wales/

CHAPTER 20

Reflections and Future Directions in Practitioner Research

Kate Mawson[a], Thomas Perry[b],
Claire Haresnape Tyson[c] and
Joyce I-Hui Chen[d]

[a]Nottingham Trent University, UK
[b]University of Warwick, UK
[c]Homewood School and Sixth Form Centre, UK
[d]College of West Anglia, UK

Themes and Challenges Emerging from This Collection

In drawing this guide to a close, we reflect on the themes, insights, and tensions that have emerged across its chapters. Together, they offer a compelling vision of practitioner research (PR) as a powerful mode of professional inquiry – one that repositions educators as researchers and schools as knowledge-generating institutions.

Teaching is more than the delivery of a curriculum; it is an intellectual and ethical pursuit requiring constant inquiry. PR brings teachers into the role of knowledge creators, fostering a critical, systematic approach to pedagogy and student learning. As demonstrated throughout this book, PR holds democratic potential: it values the lived experiences of teachers, elevates their insights, and promotes contextually relevant solutions to complex educational challenges.

Yet, PR is not without struggle. Structural constraints such as time, funding, and recognition continue to limit its potential. The dual role of the teacher as both practitioner and researcher often goes unacknowledged in formal systems. These tensions highlight persistent inequalities in whose knowledge is recognised, legitimised, and used to shape the future of education.

What We Have Learned

Having explored diverse perspectives on PR throughout this volume, we now offer a synthesis of the key insights that have emerged. These themes reflect the evolving nature of PR, the tensions that shape its practice, and the opportunities it presents for professional learning and educational change. Together, the contributions present a compelling vision of PR as a powerful form of professional inquiry – one that repositions educators as knowledge producers and schools as sites of knowledge generation.

Teaching is not simply the delivery of curriculum; it is a professional and ethical practice grounded in inquiry. PR enables educators to generate knowledge through systematic investigation of their own contexts. It offers democratic potential by valuing teacher expertise, elevating lived experience, and generating locally grounded responses to complex educational challenges.

In her chapter on initial teacher education, Vicky Christoforatou argues that PR should be embedded early in a teacher's formation. Rather than focusing solely on mastering prescribed pedagogies, she advocates for inquiry-based training, where new teachers are encouraged to question, investigate, and refine their practice. This approach aligns with a teacher-as-researcher tradition that reaffirms the role of educators as agents of knowledge, not merely implementers of it.

Marsden and Peiser's analysis of research-engaged schools highlights the influence of institutional culture on PR. Their vignettes illustrate how some schools foster inquiry and professionalism, while others impose constraints due to workload, performativity, or limited leadership support. The contrast they present demonstrates how enabling structures can deepen teachers' sense of agency and their engagement with research.

Despite its benefits, PR often lacks formal recognition within policy and academic contexts. Adriane Martini identifies a persistent hierarchy in knowledge production, where academic research is legitimised through funding and publication, while PR is undervalued and often unsupported. While some contributors celebrate its growing legitimacy, Martini's critique reminds us that without funding, time, and career pathways, teacher-led inquiry remains precarious. Many teachers conduct research in addition to full-time responsibilities, which restricts its sustainability and impact.

A recurring thread across the volume is how power and positionality shape the process and impact of PR. By inviting teachers to investigate their own practice, PR fosters a more democratic, grassroots approach to knowledge production. Yet as several authors show, this also introduces complexity. Sarah Peters and Joyce I-Hui Chen explore the ethical dilemmas of insider research – particularly when educators navigate dual roles as teacher, colleague, and researcher. They stress the importance of transparency, reflexivity, and care in managing role conflicts and power dynamics.

Sylvia Ikomi's chapter demonstrates how PR can illuminate systemic injustices, such as the adultification of Black girls in disciplinary practices. Her work shows how identity powerfully shapes the questions researchers ask, the interpretations they make, and how their findings are received. Her positionality as a Black woman educator is not just context – it is central to the research process and its potential for transformative impact.

Marsden and Peiser return to the politics of legitimacy, noting that teachers often feel they must 'prove' the value of their research, especially in systems where evidence is defined by policy mandates or performance data. In contrast, Peters and Chen suggest that PR can be a space of resistance, enabling educators to advocate for alternative, locally responsive approaches to improvement. This tension between imposed standards and professional inquiry emerges as a defining feature of the landscape.

Taken together, the contributions in this volume challenge dominant narratives and expand the parameters of educational research. PR, as shown here, is not ancillary – it is integral to how we understand, shape, and renew our education systems.

Bridging Theory and Practice

A key strength of PR lies in its capacity to bridge the persistent gap between academic theory and the lived realities of classroom practice. Many chapters in this volume explore how teacher-led inquiry enables educators to adapt and critically engage with research within their own contexts, making theory not only accessible but responsive to real-world conditions. Rather than viewing research as something abstract or external, these contributions highlight how teachers actively shape, test, and refine ideas through situated inquiry.

Holly Heshmati argues that practitioner researchers inhabit a unique space at the intersection of knowledge production and application. They are both generators and users of knowledge – translating theory into pedagogical strategies, refining frameworks through iterative practice, and generating insights that speak directly to the challenges of teaching and learning. Building on this perspective, Adriane Martini explores the role of knowledge brokers and professional learning networks in enhancing the reach of PR. Her chapter makes the case for more deliberate mechanisms to support the translation and dissemination of findings – such as digital platforms, school-based research hubs, and inquiry-led collaborations that extend beyond the individual classroom.

This emphasis on communication and impact is echoed in other contributions, which stress that PR gains momentum and legitimacy when it is embedded in collective structures. Frances-Ann Norton's chapter highlights the importance of collaboration through communities of practice, where teachers co-construct knowledge, share interpretations, and offer mutual support. She illustrates how inquiry groups and teacher learning communities foster sustained professional growth by creating spaces for reflection, dialogue, and experimentation.

Yet, this collaborative vision is not without its constraints. Martini's critical perspective reminds us that institutional support for PR is often limited or inconsistent. Despite its transformative potential, PR is frequently conducted in marginal time – outside timetabled hours, with limited access to resources or recognition. In such conditions, collaboration becomes difficult to sustain. Without protected time, leadership endorsement, or systemic integration into professional development frameworks, even the most promising inquiries risk becoming isolated efforts rather than catalysts for lasting change.

Taken together, these chapters offer both inspiration and provocation. They celebrate the ingenuity and professionalism of teachers who engage in inquiry, while also drawing attention to the structural and cultural conditions that shape what is possible. If PR is to achieve its full potential, it must be supported by systems that recognise its value – not only in terms of outcomes, but as a vital mode of professional agency and educational improvement. The interplay between individual initiative and institutional support emerges as a central tension – and a crucial area for future development.

Methodological and Epistemological Tensions in PR

A deeper issue underlying the uncertainties around PR is the question of what counts as credible, rigorous inquiry. Throughout this volume, contributors highlight the ongoing tension between flexibility and methodological robustness. Holly Heshmati's discussion of pragmatist approaches illustrates how PR often blends qualitative, quantitative, and mixed-methods traditions, drawing flexibly from what best suits the context. This methodological pluralism is part of PR's strength, allowing it to remain responsive and adaptive to practice-based needs. Yet, as others note, this flexibility can also invite scepticism – particularly when there is no shared framework for evaluating quality, reliability, or ethical practice.

The question of what constitutes 'good' PR remains unresolved. While approaches such as action research are widely used, there is little consensus around the standards or criteria that should guide PR. For some, rigour is defined through formal ethics approval, peer-reviewed dissemination, and structured methodological design. For others, rigour lies in reflexivity, contextual fit, and practitioner utility. This tension reveals a deeper debate: should PR conform to the expectations of academic research, or should it develop its own criteria grounded in practice-based credibility?

Issues of positionality and subjectivity further complicate the methodological landscape. Sarah Peters and Joyce I-Hui Chen explore the ethical dilemmas inherent in insider research, where practitioners investigate their own communities. Their chapter highlights the importance of maintaining a critical stance, acknowledging the risk of confirmation bias, and carefully navigating the overlapping roles of teacher, colleague, and researcher. They emphasise that PR must go beyond affirmation, and instead embrace discomfort, critique, and ethical complexity.

Sylvia Ikomi's contribution extends this conversation by showing how PR can challenge dominant knowledge systems. Her inquiry into the adultification of Black girls in school disciplinary practices foregrounds the significance of researcher identity – not just as background context, but as a central feature of knowledge production. Like Peters and Chen, Ikomi invites us to take seriously the implications of conducting research from within, especially when lived experience and social identity intersect with systems of oppression. These accounts complicate assumptions about objectivity, showing that subjectivity and embeddedness can offer depth, insight, and transformative potential – if approached with reflexivity and rigour.

The challenge of sustaining and scaling PR also surfaces repeatedly across the volume. Frances-Ann Norton reflects on the highly localised nature of much PR – often conducted by individuals or small teams within a specific school context. This local relevance is a strength, but it can limit broader influence. To address this, several authors argue for more robust dissemination strategies and infrastructure. Martini's work on knowledge brokers and professional learning networks suggests that intermediary actors can help extend the reach of PR, translating its findings for wider audiences and shaping institutional cultures of inquiry.

Yet scaling PR is not simply a technical task – it also requires memory, continuity, and leadership. Marsden and Peiser's study of school-based research cultures highlights a common problem: when key research-active staff leave, the momentum often dissipates. Without systems to embed PR into school structures, inquiry tends to be episodic and person-dependent, rather than sustained and strategic.

A final uncertainty concerns PR's capacity to influence policy. Despite its depth and relevance, practitioner-generated knowledge remains largely absent from national policy discourse. Martini's critique points to an entrenched preference for large-scale studies, government-led initiatives, and external evaluation frameworks. In this context, PR is frequently overlooked – not because it lacks value, but because it does not easily fit prevailing models of evidence. Without systemic advocacy and structural change, PR risks being perceived as valuable within classrooms but inconsequential at the system level.

Moving Forward

Having explored both the strengths and uncertainties of PR, we now consider what is needed for it to gain greater legitimacy, impact, and sustainability. While this book has illustrated the significant potential of PR to improve teaching and learning, it has also revealed enduring barriers – among them a lack of time, recognition, and structural support. Moving forward requires a shift in how we conceptualise, fund, and embed PR: not as an optional add-on, but as an essential element of professional practice.

A key issue is the limited capacity many teachers have to engage meaningfully in research. Without formal training in methods or sustained professional development, PR can remain fragmented and informal. Vicky Christoforatou argues that inquiry should be central to initial teacher education, not peripheral. This involves introducing research literacy as a core component, offering structured inquiry opportunities for trainees, and developing mentoring frameworks where experienced teacher-researchers guide early-career colleagues. Marsden and Peiser echo this view in their analysis of research-engaged schools, noting that even experienced educators struggle to access high-quality CPD focused on inquiry. Strengthening methodological confidence and embedding PR into CPD pathways are thus essential steps.

Time remains one of the most frequently cited obstacles. Teachers often undertake research in their own time, without protected space or workload recognition. Addressing this requires a systemic commitment: schools and trusts can create designated research roles, integrate inquiry time into teachers' working hours, and develop partnerships with universities to support teacher-led research. Such changes would move PR from a peripheral activity to a recognised aspect of professional contribution.

Recognition also remains a central concern. PR is often undervalued when compared to traditional academic outputs, especially within policy and funding frameworks. The concept of the 'pracademic' – someone who moves fluidly between practice, policy, and research – offers a powerful way of rethinking legitimacy. By framing PR as a hybrid professional space, institutions can move beyond binary models and create roles, incentives, and pathways that support teacher-researchers. Hollweck, Netolicky, and Campbell's work provides a strong theoretical foundation for this reimagining.

Access to funding is another critical lever. As Adriane Martini notes, PR is rarely prioritised by formal funding bodies, which continue to favour large-scale academic research. Targeted grants, institutional research budgets, and national funding streams specifically for teacher-led inquiry could provide a foundation for more equitable participation in research. Alongside this, there is a need to open up new dissemination pathways. Many PR findings remain within individual schools. Digital platforms, regional research hubs, and expanded opportunities for teachers to present at conferences would help raise the visibility and influence of their work.

Collaboration is consistently identified as one of PR's greatest strengths and greatest challenges. Frances-Ann Norton highlights the value of peer learning communities and cross-school collaborations, but also notes that sustained collaboration depends on time, leadership, and structure. Marsden and Peiser show that when research is embedded within the school culture, and when teachers work collectively, its impact can scale. Formal networks at local, regional, and national levels – as well as co-led projects between schools and universities – are critical to making PR sustainable.

Universities must also reassess their role in partnerships. Martini points out that many collaborations remain one-sided, with universities as knowledge producers and schools as consumers. A more equitable model would support teacher-led research in HE settings, provide joint supervision or funding schemes, and establish research fellowships that cross institutional boundaries. These partnerships could also help address the methodological tensions raised by Heshmati by offering teachers guidance while respecting their autonomy.

If PR is to become a core feature of the teaching profession, its value must be embedded in the culture and career structures of schools. Several chapters in this book highlight the long-standing division between research and teaching – a divide that has limited how teaching is perceived and rewarded. This division must be challenged. Professional standards can play a role by explicitly recognising research engagement; so too can career progression frameworks that reward inquiry as a marker of leadership and expertise. As Marsden and Peiser argue, when PR becomes part of the everyday professional landscape, it ceases to be an extra burden and becomes a route to deeper learning.

Crucially, PR must be seen not only as a school-based endeavour but as part of the broader ecosystem of education policymaking. Martini's critique underscores how teacher-led insights are largely absent from national debates, which continue to be shaped by external evaluations and top-down agendas. To address this, policymakers should engage directly with PR communities. Networks of practitioner-researchers could produce briefings, consultations, or position papers that bring grounded insights into policy spaces. Government agencies can also play a role by establishing mechanisms to integrate PR into formal decision-making.

This book has shown that PR is a powerful tool for professional development, school improvement, and educational change. But to realise its full potential, we must build capacity through structured research training and CPD, secure recognition through funding and dissemination, and embed collaboration across schools, universities, and systems. More fundamentally, we must affirm the principle that teaching is itself a research-rich endeavour. PR cannot remain something done only by the few, in their own time, against the grain. It must be enabled, expected, and embedded as part of what it means to teach well – and to lead in education.

Glossary

We collected contributions to a glossary and then sent out the glossary to contributors to promote more consistent use of terms, provide clarity and facilitate knowledge exchange. These contributions were amalgamated and then distilled down to 150 words and suggested references.

The editors provided a glossary of terms to ensure consistency and clarity across the diverse contributions from various educational settings. Given the range of contexts, terms can have different meanings depending on local educational environments. The glossary was designed to establish a shared vocabulary, ensuring contributors were aligned in their use of key terms, making the content more accessible and helping readers understand the terms within their specific contexts.

While the glossary may not fully align with the diversity of meanings attached to terms in different settings, the editors recognised that the primary goal of the book was to facilitate knowledge exchange and build communities of practice. A shared understanding of key concepts was conducive to effective communication and dialogue among contributors and readers. In this regard, the glossary prioritised coherence, ensuring the knowledge shared could be easily understood and discussed by all.

The glossary allowed contributors to define terms relevant to their specific contexts while maintaining a common language throughout the book. This was important because contributors may interpret terms differently. By offering a common reference point, the glossary facilitated alignment without overly restricting local meanings.

Ultimately, the inclusion of the glossary reflects the editors' goal of promoting meaningful knowledge exchange and fostering a collective space for dialogue and community-building. While it may limit some local nuances, it strikes a balance between ensuring a common understanding of key concepts and respecting the diversity of educational practices. In doing so, the glossary supports clarity, facilitates discussion, and helps maintain respect for the epistemic diversity of the contributors (Dr Kate Mawson, 2025).

Key Term	Definition	References
Case Study	A case study in practitioner research is an in-depth exploration of a real-life subject, such as an individual, group, event, or organisation, within a specific setting like a classroom. It allows researchers to deeply analyse teaching practices or learning environments, focusing on significant events, interactions, or decisions. Case studies are small-scale research projects aimed at answering specific questions, with the potential to be exploratory, confirmatory, or illustrative, depending on the researcher's goal. They provide 'context-dependent knowledge' (Flyvbjerg, 2004), offering insights grounded in the specific case. Though often considered a method or methodology, a case study is more accurately a heuristic device guiding inquiry across different research paradigms (Van Wynsberghe & Khan, 2007). Case studies can be conducted by practitioners or academics, or both, and may involve multiple cycles of inquiry. This approach helps practitioners reflect on their practice and share findings within the broader educational community.	Flyvbjerg, B. (2004). Five misunderstandings about case-study research. *Sosiologisk tidsskrift*, 12(2), 117–142. VanWynsberghe, R., & Khan, S. (2007). Redefining case study. *International Journal of Qualitative Methods*, 6(2), 80–94.

Close-to-Practice research	Close-to-practice research is an approach to inquiry that investigates real-world professional settings with the goal of directly informing and improving practice. Rooted in the lived experiences of practitioners – such as teachers, healthcare professionals, and social workers – this research is context-driven and seeks to make connections between theoretical knowledge and the practical challenges encountered in professional fields. Close-to-practice research is inherently collaborative, often involving partnerships between researchers and practitioners or practitioners engaging in systematic inquiry within their own professional contexts. It recognises the insider-outsider dynamic, where practitioners critically reflect on their roles as both researchers and participants, ensuring findings are both rigorous and applicable. Particularly relevant in education and healthcare, this approach fosters research that is responsive to the complexities of practice, blending teaching, research, and activism. By prioritising practitioner-defined issues, close-to-practice research strengthens the relationship between research and professional practice, enhancing both theory and application.	https://www.bera.ac.uk/publication/bera-statement-on-close-to-practice-research Wyse, D., Brown, C., Oliver, S., & Poblete, X. (2021). Education research and educational practice: The qualities of a close relationship. *British Educational Research Journal*, 47(6), 1466–1489. Brown, N., & Ergül, H. (2024). Social Fiction as a close-to-practice research approach. Wyse, D., Brown, C., Oliver, S., & Poblete, X. (2018). *The BERA close-to-practice research project: Research report*. British Educational Research Association.

(Continued)

Key Term	Definition	References
Continuing Professional Development (CPD)	Also referred to as Professional Development, Continuing Professional Development (CPD) is a structured and ongoing process through which professionals enhance their knowledge, skills, and practices over time. In the context of education, CPD enables teachers to update subject-specific knowledge, refine pedagogical approaches, and engage in reflective practice to improve teaching and learning. Unlike one-off professional development experiences, CPD is cyclical and progressive, forming part of a teacher's broader professional learning journey. It is often embedded within institutional frameworks, with dedicated time allocated for training, ensuring compliance with professional standards and educational policies. While traditionally seen as a top-down approach, often imposed on teachers with limited agency, Ur (1997) highlights an alternative experiential model that encourages active teacher engagement in their own development. Ultimately, it serves to equip educators with the necessary expertise to respond to evolving pedagogical and policy demands, ensuring effective and informed teaching practice.	Broad, J. H. (2015). So many worlds, so much to do: Identifying barriers to engagement with continued professional development for teachers in the further education and training sector. *London Review of Education*, 13(1), 16–30.

Participatory research	Participatory research is a collaborative and action-oriented methodological approach in which educators, such as teachers and lecturers, generate knowledge from their pedagogic experience. Rooted in critical qualitative methodologies, this approach actively engages practitioners and participants in the research process to effect meaningful change. Co-authors or co-participants play an integral role, contributing to both data collection and analysis, thereby ensuring that the research remains reflective of their lived experiences. This method fosters collaboration between educators and their students, as well as among practitioners, to identify and address challenges within classroom practice. By involving those directly affected by the research topic, participatory research promotes inclusivity and shared ownership of knowledge production. The ultimate objective is not only to understand educational practices but also to drive transformation, making research a vehicle for social and institutional change. This approach aligns with emancipatory research traditions, valuing the voices of participants as co-constructors of knowledge.	Park, P. (2006). Knowledge and participatory research. In *Handbook of action research* (Vol. 2, pp. 83–93). Pain, R., & Francis, P. (2003). Reflections on participatory research. *Area*, 35(1), 46–54. Durrant, K. K. (2015). *Exploring learning in practice to support construction teachers' professional development* [Doctoral dissertation, London South Bank University]. Burke, P. J. (2002). *Accessing education. Effectively widening participation*. Stoke-on-Trent, Trentham Books. Vaughn, L. M., & Jacquez, F. (2020). Participatory research methods–choice points in the research process. *Journal of Participatory Research Methods*, 1(1).

(*Continued*)

Key Term	Definition	References
Practitioner Researcher	Practitioner research is a systematic and reflective approach in which professionals integrate research into their practice to enhance their work, inform policy, and improve the experiences of learners, colleagues, and stakeholders. Rooted in action research and close-to-practice methodologies, it is undertaken by individuals who have been or remain practitioners, such as teachers, lecturers, healthcare professionals, or social care workers. Unlike teacher research, which is often classroom-focused, practitioner research extends across diverse professional settings, fostering improvements within organisations and professional fields. Reed and Procter (1995) define practitioner researchers as 'practitioners who are involved in doing research into areas of their practice'. This process involves critically examining one's own professional environment, engaging with colleagues and students as active participants, and using research to drive meaningful change. The term is inclusive of teaching assistants, higher education lecturers, and professionals in non-educational fields, ensuring a broader application beyond traditional teaching roles while maintaining a commitment to evidence-based practice and policy development.	Reed, J., & Procter, S. (1995). Practitioner research in context. In *Practitioner research in health care* (pp. 3–31). Springer US.

Professional Growth	Professional growth is a reflective and ongoing process through which educators evolve in their practice, identity, and expertise over time. Distinct from professional development, which often focuses on structured learning imposed by organisations, professional growth is an individualised journey of applying knowledge and skills to enhance teaching performance and personal fulfilment. It allows teachers the time and space – often outside contractual obligations – to engage in deep reflection, collaboration, and critical inquiry. Clarke and Hollingworth (2002) conceptualise professional growth as a non-linear process, shaped by the complex interplay between beliefs and practice. Schon (1983) similarly challenges deficit-based models, advocating for reflective growth that nurtures self-efficacy and agency. This process involves networking, observing peers, and questioning established methods to foster maturation in pedagogy. Ultimately, professional growth promotes confidence, well-being, and sustained engagement with teaching, ensuring educators continually refine their approach to support both their own development and their students' learning.	Clarke, D., & Hollingsworth, H. (2002). Elaborating a model of teacher professional growth. *Teaching and Teacher Education, 18*(8), 947–967. Schön, D. A. (2017). *The reflective practitioner: How professionals think in action.* Routledge.

(Continued)

Key Term	Definition	References
Professional Learning	Professional learning is a continuous and reflective process through which educators expand their knowledge, skills, and thinking to enhance both their own practice and student outcomes. While often used interchangeably with professional development, professional learning is distinct in its emphasis on teacher agency, ongoing engagement, and critical inquiry. It involves structured activities such as attending conferences, engaging with academic literature, and participating in courses or training sessions, which may range from practical skills development to theoretical exploration. The Institute of Educational Sciences (USA) highlights professional learning as a model that fosters both teacher and learner improvement, a stance also adopted by the Teaching Council in Scotland. Unlike one-off professional development sessions, professional learning is sometimes self-directed, allowing practitioners to explore areas of personal and professional interest. Through reflective engagement with external sources and collaboration with peers, professional learning supports educators in staying informed, adaptable, and critically engaged in their field and can be instrumental in developing a collaborative research culture.	Cordingley, P., Higgins, S., Greany, T., Buckler, N., Coles-Jordan, D., Crisp, B., & Coe, R. (2015). Developing great teaching: Lessons from the international reviews into effective professional development. https://tdtrust.org/wp-content/uploads/2015/10/DGT-Full-report.pdf

| Reflexivity | Reflexivity is a qualitative tool which accounts for how subjectivity shapes researcher inquiry. Reflexivity impacts how researchers make and communicate nuanced and ethical decisions which reflect the untidiness of participants' experiences (Finlay, 2002). This subjective outlook is embraced as part of the qualitative research process (Olmos-Vega et al., 2023). | Olmos-Vega, F. M., Stalmeijer, R. E., Varpio, L., & Kahlke, R. (2023). A practical guide to reflexivity in qualitative research: AMEE Guide No. 149. *Medical Teacher*, 45(3), 241–251.

Finlay, L. (2002) Negotiating the swamp: the opportunity and challenge of reflexivity in research practice. *Qualitative Research*, 2(2), 209–230. |

(Continued)

Key Term	Definition	References
Research-engaged practice	Research-engaged practice is an approach to teaching and professional development in which educators actively engage with research to inform, critique, and refine their pedagogical approaches. Unlike passively applying existing research, this model encourages teachers to critically question educational theories, interpret findings, and, in some cases, conduct their own systematic enquiries. It fosters a dynamic interaction between theory and practice, enriching professional judgment and decision-making. According to Chitty (2009), teacher education should immerse educators in theoretical debates, developing independent judgement rather than promoting a technical, competency-based model. Research-engaged practice aligns with this view by encouraging educators to integrate scholarly perspectives into classroom decision-making, enhancing both personal growth and institutional development. It also involves reflective practice, where teachers systematically evaluate their methodologies in response to emerging research. This approach promotes collaborative learning communities in which practitioners contribute to knowledge creation, ensuring that educational practices remain innovative, evidence-informed, and contextually relevant.	Zundel, M., & Kokkalis, P. (2010). Theorizing as engaged practice. *Organization Studies, 31*(9–10), 1209–1227. https://www.gov.scot/policies/schools/teachers/#initialeducation Tavares de Sousa, R., Lopes, A., & Boyd, P. (2020). Initial teacher education and the relationship with research: Student teachers' perspectives. *Studia Paedagogica, 25*(2), 161. Broadhead, S., & Gregson, M. (2018). *Practical wisdom and democratic education: Phronesis, art and non-traditional students.* Springer.

Research-informed Practice	Research-informed practice is an approach in which practitioners integrate established research evidence into their professional decision-making, ensuring that their methods are informed by high-quality academic studies rather than solely by tradition or experience. In education, this means that teachers actively engage with contemporary research to refine their pedagogical approaches, improve student outcomes, and enhance their own professional development. Unlike research-engaged practice, which may involve conducting original research, research-informed practice focuses on the application of existing evidence to improve teaching and learning. According to Chitty (2009) and Ur (1997), traditional teacher training often emphasises skill acquisition with limited critical reflection, whereas research-informed practice aligns more closely with teacher education, fostering a deeper, theory-driven engagement with pedagogy. By incorporating theoretical perspectives educators can critically assess and adapt research findings to their specific classroom contexts, promoting evidence-based, transformative teaching practices.	https://www.cem.org/blog/what-is-worth-reading-for-teachers-interested-in-research Flores, M. A. (2018). Linking teaching and research in initial teacher education: Knowledge mobilisation and research-informed practice. *Journal of Education for Teaching*, 44(5), 621–636. Ur, P. (1997). *The Language Teacher Online*. https://jalt-publications.org/old_tlt/files/97/oct/ur.html Chitty, C. (2009). *Education policy in Britain*. Palgrave Macmillan Nutley, S., Jung, T, & Walter, I. (2008). The many forms of research-informed practice: A framework for mapping diversity. *Cambridge Journal of Education*, 38(1), 53–71. (*Continued*)

Key Term	Definition	References
Teacher Education	Teacher education is a comprehensive and continuous process that prepares individuals for the teaching profession by integrating theoretical knowledge, pedagogical principles, and practical experience. It encompasses all activities that support both new and experienced teachers in developing their practice, expanding their pedagogical repertoire, and engaging with educational research. Unlike teacher training, which often focuses on acquiring specific competencies, teacher education adopts a more holistic approach. Chitty (2009) argues that teacher education immerses students in theoretical debates, fostering both independent judgement and intellectual engagement. This process includes postgraduate study, school placements, and professional development, ensuring that educators remain critically aware of current pedagogical topics and the complexities of learning. There has been a shift from initial teacher training (ITT) to initial teacher education (ITE), reflecting the profession's move towards lifelong learning rather than a fixed training model. Teacher education also encourages research engagement, allowing teachers to contribute to educational scholarship.	https://www.gov.scot/policies/schools/teachers/#initialeducation Sousa, T., Lopes, A., & Boyd, P. (2020). Initial teacher education and the relationship with research: Student teachers' perspectives. *Studia Paedagogica* 25(2), 161–179.

Teacher Researcher	A teacher researcher is an educator who integrates research into their professional practice, systematically investigating aspects of teaching and learning to enhance their pedagogy. While their primary role is teaching, they actively engage in inquiry, asking critical questions, challenging norms, and reflecting on their practice to improve student outcomes. Teacher researchers may conduct research within their own classrooms, drawing on qualitative and quantitative methods to examine pedagogical strategies, curriculum effectiveness, or student engagement. Ellis (2004) identifies teacher research as essential to school improvement and professional development, while Stenhouse asserts that all teachers, whether formally engaged in research or not, are inherently researchers through their ongoing reflective practice and pedagogical decision-making. The role of a teacher researcher extends beyond self-reflection to ethical research practices, data collection, and knowledge dissemination. This hybrid role fosters a culture of evidence-based practice, positioning teachers as both educators and contributors to the wider educational research community.	Ellis, C., & Castle, K. (2010). Teacher research as continuous process improvement. *Quality Assurance in Education*, 18(4), 271–285. Stenhouse, L. (1985). *Research as a basis for teaching: Readings from the work of Laurence Stenhouse.* Heinemann Educational Publishers.

(Continued)

Key Term	Definition	References
Teacher Training	Teacher training refers to the structured process by which student teachers acquire the essential skills, knowledge, and competencies required to qualify as teachers (e.g. with Qualified Teacher Status or equivalent) and become effective educators. It is typically an initial, time-limited programme that includes both theoretical learning – such as pedagogy, lesson planning, and behaviour management – and practical experience through classroom placements. Teacher training is often distinguished from teacher education, with the former prioritising the acquisition of professional skills and predetermined competencies, while the latter may encompass a broader, more reflective and research-informed approach (Chitty, 2009; Ur, 1997).	Ur, P. (1997) *The Language Teacher Online*. Chitty, C. (2009) *Education policy in Britain*. Palgrave Macmillan.
	Although the term 'teacher training' is still widely used, particularly in relation to initial teacher training (ITT), it has become less favoured in some contexts due to its implication of a finite process, rather than an ongoing professional journey. However, it remains a foundational stage in teacher preparation, equipping subject experts with the pedagogical tools necessary for effective teaching practice.	A professional programme of preparing individuals to teach in educational settings. chrome-extension:// efaidnbmnnnibpcajpcglclefindmkaj/ https://assets.publishing. service.gov.uk/ media/60e45ae4e90e0764ce826628/ ITT_market_review_report.pdf

Index

Academia, 82
Academic research, 32, 158, 194
  bridging gap between academic research and classroom practices, 33–34
Academic(s), 46
  freedom, 34
  researchers, 146
  theory, 192
Academised educational landscape, 113
Action research (AR), 71, 88, 104, 139–140, 193
  to extend critical self-reflective practice, 138–139
  inquiries, 72
  models, 92
  project, 138
Active participants, 146
Adultification, 80
Adultification-bias, 80
Affinity spaces, 36
Agency, 43, 131, 151, 191
Anonymity, 160
Anti-positivism, 15
Anti-resilient thinking, 18
Artificial intelligence (AI), 33, 36
Arts
  arts-based lecturers, 62
  arts-based research method, 40
  education, 66
  pedagogy conference, 62
Aspirational aim, 93
Assessment results, 74

Attitudes, 127
Authentic inquiry, 39

Barriers, 126, 161
Behaviours, 127, 131
Black girls, 80–81, 191, 194
Black teachers, 81, 84
Black woman educator, 191
Bridging theory and practice, 192–193
British Educational Research Association (BERA), 46, 63, 156, 158
  SIG community, 5
Broad theme for enquiry, teacher autonomy knowledge dissemination, 95–97
Burton's conceptual model, 81

Camtree, 157, 161
  digital library, 160
Classroom, 110, 112, 173
  bridging gap between classroom practices and academic research, 33–34
  practice, 96
  space, 110
Close-to-practice (CtP), 62, 68, 167, 175
  academics, 120
  develops, 62
  research, 52, 55–56, 62, 65, 66, 118
Close-to-practise research, 3
Co-constructive process, 183
Co-researchers, 131, 167

Coalescence, 118–121
Collaboration, 110, 122, 196
Collaborative act, 166
Collaborative approach, 13
Collaborative dialogue, 182
Collaborative learning, 183
Collaborative PD, 56
Collaborative practitioner research, 132
Collaborative problem-solving, 87
Collaborative process, 3, 184
Collaborative teacher groups, 94
Collaborative vision, 193
Collection, themes and challenges emerging from, 189–190
Collective autonomy, 114
Collective leadership model, 110
Communication, 118
Community, 146
  of inquiry, 64, 67
  of practice, 112, 146, 192
Complex pedagogic theory, 67
Complexity, 11
Confidentiality, 174
Confirmation bias, 194
Connecting art, 62, 66, 68
  ethics statement, 63
  pedagogic method, 63–64
  question for reader, 68
  response to editorial perspective, 68
  three lecturers, three universities, three countries, 62–63
  three sites, one method, findings/reflections, 65–66
Consortium
  coalescence, 118–121
  response to editorial perspective, 122
Constructivism, 62
Constructivist, 62
Contemporary education, 39

Content knowledge, 172
Context-sensitive approach, 13
Continuing professional development (CPD), 44, 47, 157
Core Content Framework (CCF), 26
Covid recalibration, 94
  teacher-research cycle 3, 94
COVID-19
  outbreak, 94
  pandemic, 104, 118, 139
Critical consumers of evidence, 96
Critical reflections, 77, 95–97
Critical reflective practice, 136–138
Critical self-reflective practice, action research to extend, 138–139
Critical theory, 143, 146–147, 151
  addressing power imbalances, 148–149
  applying critical theory as framework, 147–148
  participatory practitioner research, 149–151
  quality of research, 148
  question for reader, 152
  response to editorial perspective, 151
Critical thinking, 65
'Cross-flow', 97
Cross-school collaborations, 196–197
Cultivating research literacy, 88
Curriculum, 189–190
  developers, 68
  objectives, 26
  in Wales, 183
Cycle reflections, 96

Data, 129, 158, 166
  collection, 128
Day-to-day practitioners, 35
Debord's theory, 67
Deeper engagement, 39

Democratic professionalism, 136
Democratic space, 53
Department of Education (DE), 32, 140
Dérive participants drift, 64
Dewey's reflective practice, 88
Dialogical Knowledge Curation, 144, 180, 182–183, 185
    questions for reader, 185–186
    response to editorial perspective, 185
'Dialogical' component, 182
Dialogue, 166
Digital platforms, 192, 196
Disclosure, 160
'Distancing-friendly' processes, 94
Distributive leadership model, 110

Early Career Teachers (ECT), 33
Ecosystem model for collaborative problem-solving, 87
Editorial perspective, conclusion and reflection on, 75–77
Education, 11, 13, 17, 32, 140, 143, 165, 181
    context-dependent nature of, 36
    delivery, 139
    ecosystem, 103, 180
    in England, 32
    for-employment, 76
    system, 80
Education, Health and Care Plan (EHCP), 94
Education Endowment Foundation (EEF), 32
Education Inspection Framework, 73
Education Research-Practice Partnership, 118
Educational institutions, 114

Educational managers, 68
Educational policy and practice, 181
Educational research, 24, 34, 163
Educational researchers, 3, 157
Educational settings, 17
    impact of PR in, 20
Educational system, 32
Educational theory, 25
Educational values, 114
Educators, 25, 33, 36, 64, 68, 110, 112, 190
    networks, 112
Effective practitioner research, 83
Empowering staff to engage with research, 45–47
English for Speakers of Other Languages (ESOL), 71–72, 164
    pedagogy, 73
Enquiry, broad theme for, 95–97
Ethical dilemmas, 171, 175
    navigating researcher positionality and, 172–175
    questions for reader, 175–176
    response to editorial perspective, 175
Ethical research, 156
Ethics, 6–7, 57, 77
    paperwork, 174
    review committee, 158
    statement, 63
Evidence-informed practices, 13, 32
Evidence-informed profession, 43
'Evidence-informed' practitioners, 180
Exploratory practice (EP), 163
    question for reader, 168
    response to editorial perspective, 167–168
Expressive talk, 111

Facebook, 36
Fee-paying school, 47
Feedback, 95–96
   teacher-research cycle 5, 95
Fictionalising, 160
'Fiduciary relationship', 173
Formal ethics review committee, 158
Fostering research skills, 28
Further education (FE), 71
   in England elevates, 76
   sector in England, 72
   teachers, 73

Gatekeepers, 55, 76
Good-Life RealLAB, 65
'Good' quality teacher education and pedagogy, 73
Government
   agencies, 197
   agenda, 27
Group used theory, 122

Harm, 76, 160
Hermeneutic epistemology, 62
Heterogeneity, 2
Higher education (HE), 46, 51, 80, 118
   case study of PR in, 17–19
   institutions, 28, 55, 111, 149
   setting, 12, 55
Human action, 4
Human experience, 146

Identity, 79, 131
Implementation of action-research models, 92
Independent identification, 138
Individual education plans (IEPs), 44
Ingenuity, 193
Initial conceptualization, 182
Initial semi-structured interviews, 174

Initial teacher education (ITE), 88, 190
   action research to extend critical self-reflective practice, 138–139
   benefits of practitioner research in, 24–25
   conclusion and response to editorial perspective, 139–141
   critical reflective practice, 136–138
   obstacles of practitioner research in, 25–27
   response to editorial perspective, 28–
   in support of practitioner research, 136
   (unexpected) evolution of novice teacher's research role, 139
Initial teacher training (ITT), 26
   institution, 17
   process model in, 28
   stakeholders, 26
Initial wariness and resistance, 65
Innovations, 139
Inquiry
   inquiry-based training, 190
   inquiry-led collaborations, 192
   as stance, 156
Inside investigations, 72–75
Insider-researcher, 76
Insider/outsider researcher-practitioner, 171
Instagram, 36
Integrating research, 143–144

Joint Practice Development (JPD), 71, 73

Knowledge, 122, 172, 192
   broad theme for knowledge dissemination, 95–97
   broker, 35

brokering, 181–182
brokers, 194
creators, 189
curation, 182, 184
production, 62, 191
source, 113

Language
   education practitioners, 136
   teaching and learning, 163
Leaders, 94
Leadership, 94
Learners, 164, 167
   voices, 167
Learning, 95–97, 110, 126
   to teach, 101–102
Lecturers, 173
Legitimacy, 191
Limited autonomy model, 93
   teacher-research cycle 2, 93–94
Live lesson research (LLR), 52, 54
   evaluation of, 55–56
Lockdown placements, 139

Mentoring activity, 27
Mentors, 25
Mixed Methods Research (MMR), 5
Model excellent skills, 127
Mutual reciprocity, 114

National level policies, 136
Natural academic, 47
Network members, 35
New technologies, 36
Non-Black teachers, 82
Noticing, 54
Novice teachers, 137
   (unexpected) evolution of novice teacher's research role, 139

Objectives model, 26
   in ITT, 27
Objectives-based curriculum, 26

'Objectives' curriculum model, 26
Objectivism, 167
Online
   courses, 130
   roundtable discussions, 127
Open university, 119
Outstanding, 94–95
   teaching, 95
Overarching aim, 93

Pandemic, 110
Parentification, 81
Participants, 63–66, 127, 160
   participant-practitioners, 126
   participant-researcher relationships, 148
Participatory practitioner research, 149
   involving students in research, 149
   researcher positionality and bias, 149–151
Participatory research, 146, 148
Partnerships, 146, 151
Pedagogic method, 62
Pedagogical content knowledge, 172
Peer learning communities, 196–197
Peer-group mentorship program, 150
Performativity, 27
Philosophical foundations of PR, 15–17
Phronesis, 25, 63, 106–107, 121
Policy documents, 140
Policy makers, 27, 197
Positionality, 6–7, 143, 150, 191, 194
   as teacher engaging in research, 47–48
Positivism, 146
Post-cycle evaluations, 93, 95
Postgraduate Certificate of Education (PGCE), 23–24

Postgraduate-level assignments, 103
Power, 6–7, 111, 173
   consideration, 73
   curriculum, 112
   imbalance, 173
Power dynamics, 146
   in research, 21
Pracademic, 196
Practical reasoning, 106
Practice, 131
   communities of, 21
   initiation of whole-school strategy to enhance practice-based enquiry, 92–93
   model, 88
   practice-based inquiry, 139–140
Practitioner research (PR), 1, 4, 6, 11, 15, 25, 39, 41, 52, 83, 97, 106, 131, 143, 151, 156–157, 189–190
   action research to extend critical self-reflective practice, 138–139
   benefits in initial teacher education, 24–25
   bridging theory and practice, 192–193
   case study of PR in higher education, 17–19
   conclusion and reflection on editorial perspective, 75–77
   conclusion and response to editorial perspective, 139–141
   critical reflective practice, 136–138
   editorial perspective, 3–4
   ethics, power, and positionality, 6–7
   inside investigations, 72–75
   ITE in support of, 136
   key arguments and approaches, 156–160
   learned, 190–192
   methodological and epistemological tensions in, 193–195
   methodology, 5–6
   moving forward, 195–198
   obstacles in initial teacher education, 25–27
   philosophical foundations of, 15–17
   philosophical worldview, 4–5
   impact of PR in educational settings, 20
   practitioner-research partnerships, 111
   purpose and ethos, 2–3
   question for reader, 77
   redefining PR identity, 34–35
   SIG, 28
   themes and challenges emerging from collection, 189–190
   themes and trajectories, 7–9
   as unsettled and evolving, 7
   (unexpected) evolution of novice teacher's research role, 139
Practitioner researchers (PR), 1–2, 7, 11, 16, 39–40, 82, 106, 131, 143, 147–148, 167–168, 174–175, 192, 197
   develops, 110
   identities, 52
Practitioners, 46, 146, 184
   integrate theory, 87
Pragmatism, 11, 106
Praxis, 17
Pre-service teachers, 12
Preserve anonymity, 44
Primary classroom practitioners, 51
Primary consideration, 93

Primary school, 45, 183
    teacher, 172
Privacy, 160
Problem-solving, 164
Process model, 26
    in ITT, 28
Professional associations, 33
Professional development (PD), 32–33, 87, 92, 111, 126
    frameworks, 193
    methodology, 127–129
    projects, 110
    researcher positionality, 129–131
    response to editorial perspective, 131–132
    sample and main features of successful PD, 126–127
Professional development design, 52–53
    case study of, 52
    current landscape, 56–57
    ethics, 57
    evaluation of LLR, 55–56
    noticing, 54
    promote noticing, 54–55
    reflexivity and, 52–54
Professional identity, 80, 110–111
Professional ideology of practice, 157
Professional inquiry, 189–190
Professional knowledge, 45
Professional learning, 87, 92, 98, 140
    organizations, 96
    and skills, 112
Professional learning networks (PLNs), 35, 194
Professional practice, 114
Professional standards, 197
Professionalism, 48, 190, 193
Professionals, 35
Progressive learnings, 94

Promote noticing, 54–55
Pseudonyms, 44, 160
Publication, 157

Qualitative data, 43, 74
Quality of life, 164
Quantitative evidence, 74
Quantitative information, 75
Questioning approach, 102–103
'Quite unnerving', 184

Radical improvements, 32
Radical transformation, 32
Randomised controlled trial (RCT), 105
Re-evaluating, 77
Re-visiting, 77
Readers, 12
Reality shock, 32
Reconnaissance, 96
Reflective practice, 102, 136–137
    encourages self-critical engagement, 137
Reflexive account, 20
Reflexive act, 53
Reflexive interviewing, 55, 57
Reflexivity, 7, 150
    and PD design, 52–54
Relativism, 167
Research
    activity, 136
    cycle, 20
    empowering staff to engage with, 45–47
    engagement, 43, 48
    evidence, 102, 136
    involving students in, 149
    knowledge, 28
    literacy, 140, 195
    positionality as teacher engaging in, 47–48
    practitioners, 79
    process, 74
    research-engaged practice, 63
    research-engaged practitioner, 136

research-engaged schools, 190, 196
research-informed practitioner, 136
research-practice partnership, 118
research-related training practitioners, 182
school, 45, 47
skills, 138
stance, 156
subjects, 129
work, 182
Research-Informed Approaches to Tackling Educational Disadvantage (RATED), 120
consortium, 87, 118
Research-informed practices, 32, 87
bridging gap between academic research and classroom practices, 33–34
new technologies and social media, 36
PLNs and knowledge broker, 35
redefining practitioner research's identity, 34–35
three possible directions, 34
Research-informed trainee teachers
learning to teach, 101–102
response to editorial perspective, 106–107
situational verification by trainee teachers, 102–105
Researched practice, 159
Researcher, 46
identifying as, 44–45
identity, 194

Researcher positionality, 129–131
and bias, 149–151
navigating, 172–175
Resilience-building interventions, 18
Respect, 174
Resulting evidence, 136
Rewards-based behaviour system, 104
Robust research culture, 151
Roundtables, 129
Rumworth school, 92

Sampling approach, 127
Scepticism, 193
School(s), 92, 196
based research hubs, 192
closures, 118
culture, 197
foster inquiry, 190
leaders, 96
level policies, 136
organisation and management, 92
school-based endeavour, 197
school-based interventions, 88, 103
school-based research cultures, 195
school-wide feedback practices, 95
sector, 93
Secondary school, 44
teacher, 34
Self-actualisation, 113
Self-discovery, 138
Self-improving education ecosystem, 107
system, 102
Self-reflection, 150
Self-sustaining, 93
Senior Leadership Team (SLT), 92
Senior Lecturer Practitioner in Education, 172
Sharing learning, 157

Sharing practitioner research, 161
Situational verification by trainee teachers, 102–105
Small-scale research project, 164
Social climate, 83
Social interactions, 146
Social media, 36, 44
Social work research, 150
"Speaking out", 164
Special educational needs and disability (SEND), 44, 88, 92, 97
  covid recalibration, 94
  critical reflections and learnings, 95–97
  feedback, 95
  initiation of whole-school strategy to enhance practice-based enquiry, 92–93
  limited autonomy model, 93–94
  response to editorial perspective, 97–98
  teaching-observation redesign, 94–95
  total autonomy model, 93
Spousification, 81
Staff meetings, 47
Stakeholders, 55, 83
'Stereotype anxiety', 119
Students, 111–112
  teaching, 172
Subjective research process, 129
Subjectivity, 194
Successful PD, 130–131
  sample and main features of, 126–127
Sussex University, 121
Sustainable research process, 164
Sustained professional development, 195
Systematic inquiry, 102
Systemic injustices, 191
Systemic power dynamics, 147

Talk Pedagogy, 183
Taskscape, 63
Teacher-research cycle
  covid recalibration, 94
  feedback, 95
  limited autonomy model, 93–94
  teaching-observation redesign, 94–95
  total autonomy model, 93
Teacher(s), 33, 72, 120, 131, 137, 140
  agency, 48
  bias, 120
  broad theme for teacher autonomy, 95–97
  education, 34
  educator(s), 17, 23, 102, 106, 120, 140
  group of, 113
  positionality as teacher engaging in research, 47–48
  as researcher, 21
  researchers, 24, 43, 121
  resilience, 18
  teacher-enquir, 95
  teacher-research model, 88
  teacher-researcher, 174
  training, 27, 103
  voice, 96
Teacherled model, 93
Teachers teaching teachers
  my identity and my work, 80
  response to editorial perspective, 83–84
  teaching black teachers, 80–82
  teaching teachers, 82–83
Teaching, 126, 173, 189–190
  black teachers, 80–82
  profession, 197
  quality, 95
  teachers, 82–83, 102
Teaching and Learning Community (TLC), 110–111

Teaching assistants (TAs), 44
Teaching learning and assessment (TLA), 73
Teaching-observation redesign, 94, 96
  teacher-research cycle 4, 94–94
Technical task, 195
21st-century teacher, 136
Theoretical education method, 62
Third space, 118, 185
'Tokenistic' approach, 148
Total-autonomy, 93
  model, 93
  teacher-research cycle 1, 93
Toxic working culture, 82
Traditional academic systems, 149
Traditional positivist
  approaches, 146
  models, 143
Traditional research, 20
Trainee teachers, 28, 102, 106
  situational verification by, 102–105
Trainee(s), 107
  primary school teacher, 103
Transformative endeavour, 41
Transformative learning, 137

Transformative professional development, 39
Translating theory, 192
Transparency, 159
Trust, 174, 196

UK Research and Innovation (UKRI), 151
'Unbiased' lens, 74
Universities, 197

Value education, 73
Virtual meetings, 119
Voluntary informed consent, 159

Whole school teacher-research model, 92
Whole-school strategy to enhance practice-based enquiry, initiation of, 92–93
Workability, 96
Working, 127
Workplace issues, 74
Workshop, 63

X, 36

Young children, 172

www.ingramcontent.com/pod-product-compliance
Lightning Source LLC
Chambersburg PA
CBHW061937220426
43662CB00012B/1942